Dave Armstrong

Family Matters: Catholic Theology of the Family

Abortion
Contraception
Extramarital Sex
Divorce
Homosexuality
Radical Feminism

© Copyright 2007 by Dave Armstrong

All rights reserved.

Biblical citations are taken from the Revised Standard Version of the Bible (© 1971 by Division of Christian Education of the National Council of the Churches of Christ in the United States of America); unless otherwise noted.

ISBN 978-1-4303-2110-1

Cover design by Chad Toney.

For related reading on the author's blog, see:

Life Issues: Abortion, Euthanasia, Contraception

http://socrates58.blogspot.com/2006/11/life-issues-abortion-euthanasia.html

Sexuality, Gender, Feminism, & Divorce

http://socrates58.blogspot.com/2006/11/sexuality-gender-feminism-divorce.html

Liberal Theology & Modernism

http://socrates58.blogspot.com/2006/11/liberal-theology-modernism-index-page.html

DEDICATION

To Dr. James Dobson, Steve Wood, and Dr. Ray Guarendi: three Christians who have fought valiantly and eloquently in the public arena for the traditional family and Christian morality. May their important message be more widely known and received.

INTRODUCTION

The subject matter of this book is fairly self-explanatory but perhaps a brief description of my purpose is in order. My goal is simple: to present a summary of Catholic teaching on the family and sexuality, from a "lay apologetics" standpoint; and to attempt to show *why* Catholics believe as they do in these areas.

Catholics share many moral theological beliefs with our Orthodox and Protestant Christian brethren – particularly the more traditional or "orthodox" members of those communions. I rejoice in the widespread agreement on many issues, and I believe that we will affect the larger secular culture to the extent that we stand side-by-side and present a unified front.

Sometimes, sadly, there are disagreements. Contraception is the most notable instance of this. All Christian groups opposed it until 1930, when the Anglicans first allowed it, "in hard cases only." Even where such differences exist, then, arguably it is easily shown that the Catholic position was indeed the universal or overwhelmingly dominant traditional Christian position in times past. This is one of my premises.

Most Christians who are truly serious about their faith are interested in what the Church has taught through the centuries; especially what the apostles believed, and what we can learn from the Bible about morality. The present work mainly uses reason and Holy Scripture in order to explicate Catholic moral theology, in the areas of sexuality, gender, and the family. It has come about largely as a result of dialogues with those of opposing positions.

Far from being a merely "moralistic" or "puritanical" or "Victorian" sort of outlook (often perceived by many as a set of unnecessary, stifling, negative rules), Catholic moral theology is based on what God has revealed to us in His inspired Word, the Bible, and is a positive teaching about who man is, and what fulfills him, in accordance with God's purpose for His children, made in His image.

Wherever there are "rules" and "do's and don'ts," we may be confident that they are for our own good, to make us truly happy and joyful, and to achieve that inner peace which only comes from following God wholeheartedly. God knows best, with regard to what makes us happy.

The flesh often wars against the spirit, but the Holy Spirit within the Christian and the power of the sacraments to give us grace in order to live righteously, are more than sufficient (Philippians 4:13) to enable us to live in a way that will not only make us happier and more fulfilled, but also provide a witness to others that being a Christian is a joyful, not a miserable thing. Joy is not the absence of suffering, but a realization that we are where God wants us to be: doctrinally, morally, and spiritually.

It is my hope and prayer that this book will help Catholics to better understand the rationale behind their own Church's sometimes difficult-to-live-out beliefs concerning personal and institutional morality, and aid non-Catholics in finding common ground with Catholic moral teaching, and to better appreciate it, even where they find themselves in disagreement.

CONTENTS

Dedication..3
Introduction...4

1. Abortion...7
2. Contraception...25
3. Chapter Three: Extramarital Sex.......................41
4. Chapter Four: Divorce..61
5. Chapter Five: Homosexuality.............................67
6. Chapter Six: Radical Feminism..........................77

Appendix One: G.K. Chesterton on Sex and Contraception...87

    The Surrender Upon Sex
    Babies and Distributism
    Sex and Property
    Social Reform Versus Birth Control

Appendix Two: G.K. Chesterton on the Family...............107

    On Certain Modern Writers and the Institution of the Family
    The Free Family
    The Wildness of Domesticity
    The Emancipation of Domesticity

Appendix Three: G.K. Chesterton: The Superstition of Divorce
....129

Appendix Four: 1930 Lambeth Conference of Anglican Bishops: Resolutions : *The Life and Witness of the Christian Community -- Marriage and* Sex.............................143

Appendix Five: Subsequent Lambeth Conferences on Divorce, Contraception, Extramarital Sex, Homosexuality, the Ordination of Women, and Euthanasia..149

Appendix Six: Official Statements of Various Christian Denominations in Support of the Right to Abortion............155

Chapter One

Abortion

Jeremiah 1:5 "Before I formed you in the womb I knew you, and before you were born I consecrated you; I appointed you a prophet to the nations."

Psalm 139:13-16 For thou hast possessed my reins: thou hast covered me in my mother's womb. I will praise thee; for I am fearfully and wonderfully made . . . My substance was not hid from thee, when I was made in secret . . . Thine eyes did see my substance, yet being unperfect; and in thy book all my members were written, which in continuance were fashioned, when as yet there was none of them. (KJV)

Luke 1:15 . . . he will be filled with the Holy Spirit, even from his mother's womb. [referring to John the Baptist]

Luke 1:41,44 And when Elizabeth heard the greeting of Mary, the babe leaped in her womb . . . "For behold, when the voice of your greeting came to my ears, the babe in my womb [John the Baptist] leaped for joy."

God "knows" people before they are conceived because He is omniscient. He knows everything: past, present, and future, and they are all "now" to Him, because He is outside of time. So it is irrelevant from God's perspective (in terms of His knowledge of them) *when* someone is conceived. He doesn't "start knowing" them then because there is no sequence in time for Him in the first place. Jeremiah 1:5 and Psalm 139:13-16 are instances of such foreknowledge, expressed in typically Hebraic or Semitic literary form.

Predestination or foreordination is also indicated ("I consecrated you; I appointed you"; "in thy book all my members were written"). This precedes actual *existence* of a person (by its very nature). God can and does foreordain or predestine people from eternity. Many Catholic theologians believe that God includes a taking into account of what they would do under any given real or hypothetical ("middle knowledge") circumstances (the theological position known as "Molinism"). But Catholics – over against Calvinists -- deny that God predestines people to hell from all eternity, or after the fall of Man in the Garden of Eden.

Many question whether the above verses are literal or metaphorical; clearly they are to be taken literally. God said that He "formed" Jeremiah, so this is historical, not metaphorical, and God can say He did it because He is involved in everything, even natural events (if only in the sense that He made them possible by creating natural laws and the properties of matter in the first place).

God "knew" Jeremiah. This, too, is a fact (within a biblical / Christian paradigm, of course), and a function of God's omniscience. Secondly, God "consecrated" the prophet Jeremiah as well. He was a holy person, and Jews and Christians believe that all sanctity, righteousness, or holiness comes from God; enabled wholly by His grace. This really happened; therefore it is clearly literal and not metaphorical.

Thirdly, God "appointed" Jeremiah as a prophet (from the human perspective, we refer to this as a "vocation" or "calling"). This occurred in history as well. Therefore the verse is obviously literal in all its aspects.

Psalm 139 reads equally literally, and there is no textual reason to interpret it other than literally and factually. The same holds for Luke 1 and the information we have about John the Baptist. The context includes prophecies of what John would do in his function as a prophet:

> . . . he will be great before the Lord, and he shall drink no wine nor strong drink . . . he will turn many of the sons of Israel to the Lord their God, and he will go before him in the spirit and power of Elijah, to turn the hearts of the fathers to the children . . . to make ready for the Lord a people prepared. (Luke 1:15-17)

Of course, one can question from the outset whether the Bible is God's revelation. That is an entirely different matter and cannot be dealt with here. But assuming it is a revelation, and inspired, we see no reason to assume that the above passages are merely "metaphorical" or symbolic and non-literal, or non-historical, so that they would have no relevance to human beings in the womb. Everything in the texts themselves suggests otherwise; particularly the fact that Jeremiah and John were real people who lived on the earth in space-time, fulfilling what was predicted of them.

The very fact that God knows (and has an ideal plan for) every person who was ever conceived or yet to be conceived, and His granting to each of them a soul upon conception, makes abortion at any stage an unthinkably evil act for the Christian (and traditional Jews, and Muslims), because it is playing God or attempting to tie the hands of God, beyond being murder (which is quite bad enough). For the Christian, conception is intimately connected with God's will and eternal purposes, as well as to the natural events that caused it to happen in the purely scientific sense.

The passages also casually assume that Jeremiah and John were the same persons before being born as they were after. They did not become persons in the second trimester or third, or after their shoulders emerged from the birth canal, as in arbitrary and absurd secularist, radical feminist, pro-abortionist ethics. They began to exist at the moment of conception.

Conception as the point of beginning for any human being is an undisputable scientific fact, and playing around with the additional "right" of becoming a "person" at some logically absurd later stage does nothing to change that fact.

Nor is the opposition to abortion on moral or humanitarian grounds an exclusively Christian notion. The pagan Greek Hippocratic Oath (one of the foundations of the ethics of modern medicine) contained a prohibition of abortion as well. All that was needed was time and the normal prenatal nutrition for Jeremiah and John in their mother's wombs to develop into (not become) Jeremiah the Prophet and John the Baptist.

And this is the basis upon which the Bible absolutely condemns abortion. It is unthinkable; an outrage. The only way it ever became thinkable at all in Christian circles is due to the watering-down of biblical authority and the liberalization of theology, so that many Christians no longer believed in the passed-down tenets of their religious system. Abortion is absolutely contrary to the Bible, the early Church, and virtually all Christians for 2000 years, save for the last 150-200 years, when theological liberalism began eroding traditional Christianity, causing a shipwreck of faith for many.

To summarize, then, the Bible definitely opposes abortion, not directly, but in a definitive indirect, or deductive fashion:

1. The preborn child is considered every bit as much of a person as the born child.

2. No distinction of identity is made between the preborn and born person (as with Jeremiah and John the Baptist).

3. God "knows" every person who ever has or ever will exist, whether yet conceived or not, and "ordains" their conception and calling.

4. The Bible condemns murder (most famously, in the Ten Commandments).

5. Murder is the wrongful, immoral taking of a human life.

6. Therefore: since the fetus is regarded as a person like any other born person, it is included in the prohibition of murder.

7. Ergo: The Bible clearly condemns abortion as murder.

 Many think that the Catholic prohibition of abortion in all cases is excessively "rigid" and inflexible. But this "hard line" is based on an inviolable principle: that each and every conceived human being has the right to life, as each is created in the image of God and in possession of infinite dignity and worth by virtue of that fact. The common exceptions of rape and incest are arguably based on pure emotionalism, rather than lucid moral thinking and true compassion.
 It matters little to the preborn child about to be torn limb from limb and slaughtered mercilessly, who his or her mother and father are, or what the circumstance of their conception was. This is simply the Golden Rule applied consistently *in utero* as well as outside. We do not solve one horrible, despicable, evil act by committing another one even more heinous and diabolical.
 Imagine, for example, a hypothetical situation where two women are pregnant, lying on the operating table. An outsider couldn't tell any difference in the babies -- all things being equal -- not knowing the circumstances in each case. The one woman loves her child because it is "wanted" and fathered by her husband. The second is the product of rape, and hence (in this mentality) has forfeited its right to live.
 Our secular society would now have us believe that it is morally defensible to go and kill the second child: to rip it to shreds with a calculated cruelty that would make a Nazi blush (even at full-term in the case of partial-birth infanticide -- of which there are about 75,000 a year), simply because of how the child came into being.
 Absolutely no moral defense can be made for such a brutal action. This sort of "morality" is no longer Christian, but rather, sheer utilitarianism and situation ethics. The traditional Christian principle is that every conceived child has an inherent

right to life, but now we chip away at that with our "exceptions" and "hard cases."

As a purely legal and pragmatic matter, it is obviously better to have laws prohibiting abortion, with these exception clauses, than the current holocaust with no limitations whatsoever, and steps ought to be taken to enact such reforms by those who can do so in good conscience.

The Catholic Church, however, cannot endorse any tenet that abandons certain preborn children to murder. No Catholic in good standing has the liberty to do that, and it would be a mortal sin. We can work on individual proposals such as the ban on partial-birth infanticides, as long as they don't entail any betrayal of our principles. In other words, there we are simply saving those children, but not abandoning others who are unfortunate enough to have the wrong parent(s). It is the *willing* of the death (whether directly or by indirect but inevitable implication) of any child that is evil.

Therefore a Catholic can't support a comprehensive law with the "hard exceptions," for that reason, although we would certainly rejoice in all the children that would live as a result of such legislation. The "exceptions" are what brought us abortion-on-demand in the first place, on the slippery slope, so I think it is foolish to believe that the same mentality will bring the slaughter to an end.

The lie and the sin is at the *root*, not out on the peripheries of this issue. Situation ethics isn't the answer; traditional Christian ethics whereby every conception is infinitely valuable and made in God's image, is the solution to our culture of death.

In the case of a woman who was raped and became pregnant, the Catholic approach distinguishes between the ethical and the pastoral. There is a real tension between them in such difficult situations as this. The woman needs to be tenderly cared for in the pastoral sense. Advocating the life of her child, on the other hand, is not motivated by a disdain for her needs in that horrible situation, but rather, doing the right thing for every person involved. Killing her own child (or allowing it to be killed) simply adds to the woman's misery. Now she has committed an evil act, and reduces herself ethically to the level of the person who violated her. Two wrongs don't make a right.

The other commonly discussed "hard case" is "the life of the mother." There are very very few situations where an abortion saves the mother's life. I once had an abortionist admit that to me face to face. If the doctor is trying to save her life and in so doing, the baby dies, he is not at fault, for he did not willfully determine to kill the child, but to save the woman's life. He willed the good, not the bad.

Ethics don't change just because there are highly charged emotions at play. The good ethicist will not allow emotionalism to make him violate ethical standards. A baby's life hangs in the balance, no matter what the circumstances are. And wantonly, deliberately slaughtering that baby is always wrong -- no exceptions. The evil lies in the evil will and malicious intent. But the killing of an innocent child is objectively evil in all circumstances.

Christians are often pilloried for trying to "force" our morality on a nation no longer consciously Christian, and on people who don't claim to be following Christian teaching at all. But we shouldn't therefore cease trying to push for pro-life legislation that is in line with Christian morality, therefore true and pragmatic, and good for the country.

There would not have been political and social moral reform in England in the early 19th century (including abolition of slavery), without the revivals of John Wesley and George Whitefield in the 18th century. The Second Great Awakening (roughly during the 1840s) played the same role in America. It's equally wrong to believe in politics as a cure-all, or to regard it as a purely pagan enterprise, not for Christians.

Society often regards law as equal to morality. When abortion was legalized, many people (not used to moral or ethical reflection) simply assumed that it was therefore moral. If sin can be sanctioned by law, why not righteousness? Babies are dying every day. This is not just an abstract consideration; it is a holocaust. The protection of the helpless innocents far overrides in importance (infinitely so) one political philosophy or moral goal as opposed to another

Christians aren't requiring people to become Christians in the case of abortion; but to merely rise to the level of civilization and the most rudimentary, obvious natural moral law. Everyone knows abortion is wrong as soon as they (hypothetically) are asked to kill *this* baby inside of *this* woman's body. If someone wouldn't squirm at that point then they are an inhuman monster.

People know murder is wrong. One doesn't have to be a Christian to know that. All societies in all periods have condemned murder. But they selectively and hypocritically apply the prohibition in most cases, as we do now with the class of the preborn human beings. We simply define them down as sub-human and barbarously and mercilessly slaughter them.

Truth is not determined by relativistic notions of pluralism. People have, of course, different views on abortion, but in any event, people still have a common sense of right and wrong, in a broad sense, regardless of their protestations to the contrary. I can think of any number of things which virtually all thoughtful people would hold to be "wrong," such as Naziism, rape, betrayal, kidnapping, incest, murder (not all particulars, but the general concept), theft, etc.

Other than on a religious or natural law basis, there are no other ways to argue the wrongness of abortion, except for perhaps the "pain" argument (which is often applied freely to animal rights issues). Or one might provide documentation concerning how abortion harms women in many ways. As Christians, we will always be opposed by the world's way of thinking. St. Paul argued with Jews and Greeks, but they largely rejected him.

The Catholic and Christian task in issues such as these -- ultimately --, is to demonstrate that the Christian outlook is the most rational, humane, and sensible view; in fact, truth itself. In doing so, we will have to defend concepts such as natural law and (if it comes to that) the validity of Christian Tradition. There is no way out of it. Otherwise, we forfeit the definition of terms and arguments to the non-believer, and this the Christian can never do.

People in reality do accept fundamental notions of moral precepts and right and wrong. If they claim they are relativists, then they always contradict themselves somewhere down the line. I have seen no exception to that rule.

In the case of abortion, for example, the typical secularist or more politically liberal (self-described "progressive") individual has all sorts of compassion for lowly animals, and the pain a beaver feels in a leg trap, etc. Catholics concur with them in that. But our goal is to show that their own principles of compassion compel them to be pro-life as well (on the rudimentary ethical basis of the pain of the preborn baby being slaughtered, if nothing else).

This (at that point) is not specifically Christian ethics; it is a challenge to be consistent with their own secular, humanist ethics. Also, the feminist should -- in all consistency -- be opposed to a forced abortion policy (China) or the practice of sex selection abortion that inevitably discriminates against female babies. And the good liberal (at least in the old definition) should oppose the killing of handicapped babies, on the basis of civil rights, compassion for the least among us, the underprivileged, etc.

One need not quote the Bible or popes, in order to argue against abortion, when dealing with people who accept the authority of neither. Pro-lifers, when dealing with secularists or nominal Christians, can utilize the pain argument, and the argument from the harm caused to women. Those things are pretty straightforward. I don't think one even needs any universal precepts to understand them. Pain is pain. Any conscious being comprehends that.

We have long since known that most babies being slaughtered feel the pain of that hideous act. We are calling for the pro-aborts to be consistent with their own principles of supposed compassion. The medical facts of development are also entirely on our side, and they aren't religiously based, either.

Oftentimes, the passion of truthtelling is pitted against the pastoral and charitable impulse. It is difficult to hold both together at the same time. But we mustn't make the mistake (as many do) of assuming that because one is passionate about evil-doing, that therefore they lack compassion for the evil-doer. Pro-lifers don't do the things they do because they hate women and want to make their life miserable. We do what we do in the way of activism because we love *both* woman and child and desired only the best for them.

We must simultaneously work to change hearts -- create a culture of life again -- and to change the law, since today people take "legal" as a synonym for "moral."

A self-consistent Christian should base his pro-life belief on religious grounds, and not be ashamed of them. If, however, we are trying to find common *philosophical* ground with non-Christians, we should usually switch over to the methodology described above. Admittedly, it is difficult to be coolly "detached" and to use "academic restraint" where matters of outrage of justice and murder of tiny children are involved. Pro-lifers are rightly emotional (or, "passionate") about it. The duty of a Christian includes rescuing the oppressed, and loving all fellow human beings. We shouldn't yield an inch to humanist principles where Christian principle is concerned.

My own pro-life convictions derive from faith and theology, no doubt, but they are not *exclusively* religious; they are also based on ethical and philosophical premises that any atheist could conceivably accept. I am convinced that I would be just as pro-life if I were an atheist, as I am now (like the well-known journalist and critic Nat Hentoff, or former abortionist Bernard Nathanson, before he became a Catholic).

I would base it on the traditional liberal / libertarian ethic of compassion for the other, the concern for the oppressed and downtrodden, and the undesirability and wrongness of pain caused to conscious creatures, as in the case of the animal rights advocates. I think pro-life flows from elementary, kindergarten ethics. Anyone who thinks it isn't elementary should be forced to observe an abortion, or at least a graphic picture of one.

We can certainly argue our pro-life case in purely secular, non-religious terms, but unfortunately, it rarely convinces anyone anyway, as there are almost always factors of the will, expedience, social pressure, and the desire for sex without responsibility involved. That's why I would look beyond even the arguing and maintain that to now defeat the abortion mentality and profitable business will require a wholesale spiritual revival.

Nothing less will fundamentally alter the status quo, and anyone who thinks otherwise is fooling themselves, I think.

We are talking about not simply human equality in this instance, but equality of all sentient creatures, at least raising humans to the level of the beasts. That's how far we have come, that one has to even argue such a manifestly evident truth. This is (in a minimalistic sense) merely self-consistent utilitarian or libertarian or classical liberal ethics, not yet necessarily requiring a Christian underpinning. Animal rights are not -- by and large -- based on Christianity, so why do fetal rights have to be? They are merely the consistent extension of the other "rights," as secular society defines them.

People who believe in absolutes are always considered arrogant and condescending and intolerant by those who are relativists or guilty of some sin being attacked, or who accept different absolutes. Christians and pro-lifers can always improve in their presentation and in the love which compels them to reach out to people with various ethical truths. I would simply add that there will always be misunderstanding and caricature and flat-out hatred of Christians. Jesus told us to expect this ("you will be hated by all for my name's sake," etc.). And what clinches that is Jesus' own story. We know He was perfect, yet we also know that He was despised, lied about, accused of being in league with Satan, of being a "wine-bibber and glutton," and ultimately betrayed, tortured and killed. All this happened to the perfect God-Man!

We should respect our hearers, our dialogical and theological opponents, and interact with them prudently and wisely. But even if we do a perfect job at that, it will not eliminate all, or even much, of the hostility against both us and our views. History bears this out quite unmistakably. And the Bible indisputably teaches it.

We can reason a pro-abortionist to pro-life entirely within the context and boundaries of their own philosophical viewpoint. Natural Law is the idea that there is an overarching morality which binds all people together. Some things are self-evident to the moral consciousness. Great works of socially-conscious literature like George Orwell's *1984* or Aldous Huxley's *Brave*

New World were based on the prior, assumed presupposition of the existence of right and wrong, and justice, and they weren't exactly evangelistic tomes.

This is a pre-Christian rationale, not a post-Christian one. Hippocrates, the pagan Greek, was pro-life, and that ethic was passed down into medicine. This is how Plato and Aristotle can be (and often are) regarded as "proto-Christians" by the Catholic Church. They had so much wisdom from natural reasoning that they often arrived at positions not dissimilar to the Christian ones, though obviously not on an overtly or self-consciously Christian basis. Likewise with today's humanists.

The question of the relationship of "human" to "person/rights" cannot be resolved rationally except to say that all of that is present from the beginning of conception. All other points are arbitrary. Science unarguably tells us when the life begins. These same "compassionate" pro-aborts and social engineers wouldn't balk for an instant if the question were about a panda egg or, say, if a dinosaur were created in some artificial womb. They would know that that life was what it was, and they would call for its protection, due to their false notion of "scarcity" as the determinant of value or worth.

They reason that since there are six billion human beings, we can dispose of *this* one -- no problem – it is better for the child, to die, for its own sake. But destroy an eagle egg or shoot a leopard, and that is a capital crime, of course! This is moral insanity. It is a *quantitative* notion of human value, rather than the *qualitative* view of Christianity (where human life; every individual person; is sacred -- infinitely valuable -- , having come from God, and made in His image).

In this mentality, it is thought that there are a lot of people around; therefore to kill some off is not only not wrong, but a positive good, as people are worth only so much as pieces of iron (which are abundant) are. If there were a thousand people in the world, then, the humanists would quickly go pro-life, as the race would be in danger of going extinct; therefore each life would become valuable (like the dodo bird or lousewort). This is Malthusianism applied to human beings.

The argument from "pain" is usually not good enough for pro-abortionists, either. They are quite content to sanction the wanton slaughter preborn babies, even up to nine months and halfway born (God help us all . . .). Life is an obvious, self-evident good; therefore pro-abortionists have to suppress their innate notions of right and wrong in order to believe in abortion as any sort of desirable "social good."

"Pain-free" or "offense-free" pro-life proclamation (like apologetics) is an impossible task. Some may delude themselves that we can engage in pro-life argumentation without causing the least offense to anyone -- so perfectly can we supposedly hone our language and approach. But we know that Jesus was perfect and He still offended people. It is a spiritual battle, not strictly an intellectual one. Many make this mistake. We are not dealing solely with intellectual "forces."

Pro-lifers have learned that we had to have much more sympathy for the woman in the crisis situation, who is ultimately a second victim in the abortion holocaust: a pawn of greedy doctor and selfish boyfriends, fathers, or husbands. We have learned that lesson long since, and it is shown in the thousands of crisis pregnancy centers, which (unlike abortion clinics) operate with no profit motive whatever.

Very few women would kill their own children without this intense pressure from ones they love, who don't really have the woman's best interests at heart, but rather, their own selfish gain and desire to flee from moral or financial responsibility, or mere embarrassment in many instances. Women have to be coerced or brainwashed by men to commit such a barbaric, unthinkable act -- against nature itself. The woman who aborts is usually a victim and a pawn.

For that reason, the woman was never punished in American jurisprudence, for abortion, as far as I know, just as we don't attempt to punish a person who tries to commit suicide (even though we have laws against it). In both cases, the person has become so victimized, and has gotten into such a crisis state, that compassion immediately comes to the forefront, superseding any thought of punishment.

The old societal pressure (much more Christian-oriented than today's society) was to be celibate before marriage, or to marry if this was not carried out and a pregnancy resulted. What a terrible, unjust world that was (so we are told)! It is hard for us these days to even imagine such intolerable repression; where men were actually coerced by societal norms to keep their pants on until they had the guts to make a marital and lifelong commitment to the woman they claim to love so much, and women realized that the gift of their intimacy and precious bodies to a mate was the most valuable possession they had, to be given out only to one who showed the utmost commitment to them. What a world!

In the pro-abortion mentality, the mother is thought to have some sort of "ownership" of another human being (like slavery). Under that assumption, the mother can do what she will. And that is why we now have sex-selection abortion, and forced abortion, as in China. In Christianity, on the other hand, murder is always wrong, because no one owns anyone else. We don't even own ourselves -- we are creatures of God: made by and for Him, which is why suicide is considered a grave sin.

Western Civilization is now a culture of death; where the most innocent and helpless among us are ruthlessly butchered and denied any semblance of human mercy and love. It is the "humanist Inquisition," so to speak. Some years ago, I came up with a semi-original proverb: "The liberalism of death is the death of liberalism."

To put it another way: the traditional self-understanding of social and political liberalism was concern for the poor, downtrodden, weak, helpless, oppressed, discriminated against, etc. (e.g., the civil rights movement, the labor movement, child labor laws, hospitals and orphanages, the New Deal, the original 19th century feminism, etc.). As such, liberalism as understood 100 years ago, was substantially in agreement with the Christian (especially Catholic ethos) of concern for one's neighbor, charity, and the "social gospel" (since distorted beyond all recognition, like its secular counterpart).

But now it isn't about that at all. The pushes towards legalized child-killing, the current acceptance of unimaginably brutal infanticide, and euthanasia and assisted suicide are all symptomatic of this transformation of liberalism into what isn't really liberalism at all, but rather, outright paganism and barbarianism (far beyond mere humanism, which is supposedly so "humanitarian").

Hitler outlawed abortion for Germans, but thought it was fine for Slavic, Gypsy, and Jewish "vermin." Many German "doctors" had already set the Holocaust mentality in motion (from the 1920s on) by concluding that there was such a thing as a "life not worthy to be lived" (e.g., the mentally ill or retarded, comatose, quadriplegic, brain-damaged, terminally ill, etc.).

In effect we (like Hitler) outlaw abortion for "wanted" children, but sanction it for handicapped ones, sometimes even wrong-sexed or freckled ones. The mother has the absolute right to dispose of her non-human "property" as she wishes. No one else has any legal say in the matter at all: not even the husband, without whom the child wouldn't be there in the first place. Our law has gone absolutely mad and schizophrenic, following our societal morality.

But in the next hospital room a more humane doctor might be taking extraordinary and technically marvelous measures to save a precious pre-natal child who has the good fortune (2 out of 3 chance) to be wanted by his or her mother. We are far worse than any pagan or barbarian society in world history, in my opinion, as we know far better, we are post-Christian, and we have both the medical and financial means to save these children from the torture and butchery they must endure.

And otherwise "respectable and decent" people will defend this savagery as a perfectly acceptable moral option! That's what is more troubling, frightening, and tragic than the most despicable example of a butcher-abortionist. He has sold his soul to the devil. But millions will defend this morally outrageous wickedness and barbarism or make it possible through their apathy. Without the acceptance of "respectable" people (including millions of professed Christians and clergy; indeed whole denominations) legal child-killing would never have gotten off the ground in this country – let alone become accepted as a matter of moronic, demonic, libertarian, political and personal expedience.

The innocent child should not be murdered in cold blood for the sake of someone else's sin and inability to control their sexual organs in an ethical and responsible fashion. Even the ancient Babylonians understood that (Code of Hammurabi). The reputable pagan Greeks did as well (Hippocrates' Oath - the "father of medicine"). Many "barbarian" Goths and others, prior to conversion to Christianity, understood it, as do many world religions. One would think that the humanist also would, given that so many are passionately concerned about slugs and trees and the possible extinction of other species -- and women's rights and children's rights and homosexual rights and minority rights and handicapped rights -- anyone but a human child. But of course we know why there is a difference: S - E - X.

I wish that just once a pro-abortionist would come out and honestly admit that legal abortion is here for one simple reason: that people want to engage in sex without restraint and responsibility -- moral principle or ethics be cursed! That would at least be refreshing, though still morally outrageous and reprehensible.

The fundamental meaning of the phrase "culture of death" is the total willingness of our humanist culture to resort to death as a perverse sort of "solution" to standard human problems. Is the baby a financial strain? Are the parents too young, or unmarried? Kill the baby. Easy solution. Quick fix. End of dilemma. Kill the child: the one party most innocent of any wrongdoing, of course. The same holds for the assisted suicide mentality, or the euthanasia mindset: kill the person going through the difficult time: don't take the self-sacrificing steps of helping them along through the difficult times or encouraging them. No: we must resort to death as the answer.

Humanist abortion is all the more heinous if it is believed that this life is all there is. Granting that false premise, the child has been deprived of virtually his or her entire life or conscious existence. How reprehensible such a view (and act) is! And yet it is upheld as moral and legally justifiable. It can't possibly be, in any sensible ethical view of any stripe, including libertarian and humanist ethics.

We have to get back to being civilized in the first place. That is where the biggest hurdle lies. The average person isn't much acquainted with philosophical ethics or Christian moral theology (let alone libertarian or humanist ethics). But they know a baby when they see one, and the bigger one is, the more undeniable that it is a (human) baby, even to a mental midget or moral moron. It's amazing what is up for debate these days.

Why should one have to argue about the evil of abortion any more than one should have to convince Hitler that killing Jews was wrong? Would anyone have even thought the latter was possible, and attempt such a thing? It is obvious that certain views are morally depraved, and as such, the holders of them are virtually immune from all moral reasoning. This is one such subject.

I don't see people passionately engaged in defending the rightness of cannibalism, or serial killers, or incest, or the savagery of the ancient Aztecs (human sacrifice) or Assyrians. Yet abortion is "respectable" in polite, academically nuanced conversation simply because it is so prevalent, as the sacrament of radical feminism and the culture of death. Ethical relativism always reduces to a head count. Once 51% of the people adopt a practice, no matter how wicked, it is then "right," because there is no higher standard by which to judge.

Chapter Two

Contraception

There is a clear moral distinction between Natural Family Planning (NFP) and contraceptives. It has nothing to do with "effectiveness." It has, on the other hand, everything to do with the will, an "anti-child mentality" and the separation of the unitive and procreative functions of marriage and sexuality. Contraception goes against natural law. NFP respects the natural order of things, especially when couples abstain during fertile periods for various reasons. To contracept is to willfully exclude the possibility of a conception and so "tie God's hands," so to speak.

Spacing of children and limiting of children for good reasons are not contraception, according to *Humanae Vitae* (the papal encyclical of 1968: "On Human Life") and Catholic moral teaching. Serious health, emotional and financial considerations were all cited by Pope Paul VI, as legitimate reasons to space or limit children. It is neither "anti-child" nor selfish for people in certain difficult circumstances to not have any further children:

> In relation to physical, economic, psychological, and social conditions, responsible parenthood is exercised, either by the deliberate and generous decision to raise a numerous family, or by the decision, made for grave motives and with due respect for the moral law, to avoid for the time being, or even for an indeterminate period, a new birth.

(*Humanae Vitae*, 10)

The willful act of seeking to prevent a possible conception by deliberate frustrating of God's possible purpose of conception is where the wrongness of artificial contraception lies. Every marital act must be open to possible conception. On the other hand, to abstain from the fertile periods involves no separation of the unitive and procreative functions, because couples are abstaining from the unitive function as well, thus honoring the coherence of the two.

To not engage in intercourse for morally acceptable reasons is essentially different than engaging in intercourse with the express purpose of frustrating the procreative potential, because the sin is not in the licit limiting of children (Catholics aren't obliged to have 12 kids!), but rather, in the deliberate, willful prevention of conception by contrived, unnatural means.

And we see the fruit of such sin in the clear correlation between contraception and abortion in virtually all the non-Muslim countries of the world. Contraception implies a radical individualism, rather than a bowing to the natural law of God. This individualism and the mindset that produces it leads -- in sinful minds -- to the notion that the terminating of a newly-conceived life is permissible. It's all diabolically consistent. Catholics see the link and so have maintained the traditional Christian prohibition. We strike at the heart and root of the problem: an anti-child, sexually liberal attitude whereby free sex and convenience is placed on a higher level than human life itself.

No Christian group accepted the moral legitimacy of contraception until 1930, when the Anglicans adopted a limited acceptance of it, in their Lambeth Conference. From that time, due to the influence of people like Margaret Sanger, who founded Planned Parenthood (and who was neck-deep in Nazi-type eugenics), radical feminism in general, and the sexual revolution of the 1960s (and – I would add -- an excessively materialistic and narcissistic brand of "Baby Boomer" capitalism), there has been a steady push worldwide (with notable exceptions, such as within Islam) to have less children and to promote contraception.

This is, frankly, an "anti-child mentality." Let's call a spade a spade. And virtually all Christian groups (except the Catholic Church) have enthusiastically joined in this irrational, utterly non-Christian denigration of children, and the formerly self-evident biblical notion that children were a blessing. The sanction of religion was absolutely necessary for the nearly worldwide triumph of contraception and legal abortion to occur.

One hears arguments about the industrial revolution, urbanization, etc., and the relationship of those societal trends to family size. These analyses are not without value on a sociological level, yet what we are seeing today goes far beyond that. Formerly "Christian" countries aren't even replacing their populations.

I used to have a delivery route in the third-richest county in the country. I saw huge houses everywhere (what used to be called "mansions"), and I knew full well that most of them are inhabited by only one child, maybe two (or none at all). I regard that as a sad visual image for what our society has become. When I grew up in a large city in the 60s, precisely the opposite held true: we had fairly small houses with many children. Even then, three or four (occasionally five) children per family was commonplace.

In my parents' generation, one can readily observe the vast demographic difference: my father came from a family of six; my wife's parents came from families of five and six. My mother was an only child, but that was because of medical problems my grandmother had. I used to be teased at work because I had three boys (since joined by a baby sister), as if that is a huge, unreasonable amount. One female professed Christian co-worker said I should get "fixed," and I'm sure she was only half-joking.

This is how low we have sunk, and it is absolutely commonplace: an unexamined assumption and presumption. Many couples today deliberately decide to not have children. In the Catholic Church, part of the marriage vows is a promise to bear children. I believe that is the case in many Protestant ceremonies also.

Such prevalent attitudes are not without serious societal and demographic effect. How could they not be, as ideas have consequences? It does not *necessarily* follow -- strictly logically speaking -- that a "contraceptive mentality" will lead to an "abortion mentality." But there is a definite connection, particularly when one looks at reproductive and abortion statistics on a nationwide and worldwide basis.

It has been shown that in every case, a nation that legalizes contraception will soon legalize abortion. It took only ten years in America. I think it was the Griswold case (c. 1963) that dealt with private use of contraception. This was the predecessor to Roe v. Wade, as I understand it, so that even in a legal sense, the connection between contraception and abortion is clear. "Progressive" judges utilized the precedents of this case in order to sanction and legalize abortion and create a right where none had previously existed. And of course, most Christian bodies had already caved on contraception, so the social progressives could co-opt and appeal to them for their essentially non-Christian, radically secularist purposes.

So what does it take for people to see the connection? The birth control pill became widespread starting around 1960. The push for abortion began in earnest by the mid-60s, becoming almost a consensus by the late 60s and early 70s. Is all this "circumstantial evidence" purely coincidental and of no import? Chronologically, legally (and I would say philosophically), the progression is evident for all to see, in my opinion.

Abortion could never have become legal in 1973 in America if it weren't for the weakness and compromise of Christians (including millions of Catholics, most notably dissident bishops). And it would have remained unthinkable but for the rapid rise of contraception. For that ushered in the utterly anti-Christian idea that one's body was one's own (as opposed to God's -- the same idea behind assisted suicide today), and that sex had no intrinsic relationship to childbearing.

Men and women could frustrate the very "hand of God," prohibit conception by a deliberate act of the will, and go ahead and engage in sex anyway. That was always regarded as pure paganism and debauchery in the Church, until 1930. And of course it has greatly promoted sexual hedonism, fornication, adultery et al, because the risks of pregnancy were reduced almost to nil. The radical feminists -- seeking to emulate the men they despised -- liked contraception because it allowed them not to be in "bondage" to children and the sexual power plays and irresponsibility of men. Abortion became their "sacrament" because it allowed them to maintain the illusion that men and women are not distinct biologically (and psychologically), by God's decree.

Yet Christians continue to fail to see the connection. In basically 40 years' time, most Christians on the earth (this includes the 70% of Catholics who contracept) adopted a practice that was previously universally condemned by Christians; one that was regarded as "murder" by Martin Luther and John Calvin (going beyond even the Catholic position). We have stopped having children, and Christians have bought this pessimistic, nihilistic, creation-hating philosophy. If only the "conservative," "traditional," "orthodox" Christians had simply continued in the traditional Christian view on this, and contined to "be fruitful and multiply," we could have transformed the world in a generation or two. As it is, Islam will now become the dominant world religion, since it still values procreation and children.

Now, I hasten to add that I wish not to condemn any *individual*. These are general philosophical, sociological and ethical observations. As in my own past history, I would suspect that most who contracept have never given a moment's thought to analyses such as these. We all have to continually educate ourselves and understand both Christian thinking and Christian history. Only then can we overcome the fads and fashions of the age and stand out as different in the eyes of the world we are only too eager to be a part of, rather than a witness and a sign of hope and transcendence.

I have two questions for those Christians who accept the moral propriety of contraception:

1) Is it really plausible and likely (let alone possible) that the entire Christian Church, in all its branches, could have gotten a moral teaching wrong for its whole history up until 1930? One could, I suppose, dismiss this difficulty by taking a position that Church history and the beliefs of the mass of Christians, Church Fathers, saints, doctors, Protestant Reformers, great pastors and evangelists, Councils, etc., are entirely irrelevant to Christian truth, but I think most knowledgeable Christians would be reluctant to take that avenue.

2) Is there another example of a teaching that was botched for 1900 years, and then the "light" went on and the Church came to its senses and got "reasonable"? A cynic might add that with regard to the Anglicans in 1930, the societal context (in England) was one of rapid secularization, religious nominalism, moral relativism, increasing sexual laxity, rampant spiritualism, Fabian socialism, head-in-the-sand pacifism (soon manifested in the Chamberlain appeasement mentality), etc. (in other words, the trend was overwhelmingly away from traditional, orthodox Christianity). One need only read Chesterton or C.S. Lewis (who were opposing it) to realize the English mindset in that period (a lot like ours in America today). Strictly from a sociological perspective, this is not an environment in which one would expect a shining new revelation of Christian truth!

I will anticipate one reply: that this itself is not an argument per se for or against contraception. I agree, strictly speaking. Yet for one who values Church history at all, and who realizes that Christians are not isolated, atomistic individuals, "condemned" to come up with all theological truth on their own apart from the witness of millions of their brethren in the faith (e.g., Hebrews 11:1-2; 12:1; Jude 3), such considerations ought to be highly troubling.

The irony and utter implausibility and "historically illogical" nature of all this is compounded when one considers how Catholics are routinely (and falsely) accused of "introducing" doctrines late (for example, the Assumption, the Immaculate Conception, papal infallibility), which are thought of as "late" or "novel" merely because they were *dogmatically defined* late (a very important distinction). That is believed to be a self-evident argument against the Catholic Church, yet it is easily and adequately explained by the notion of development of doctrine.

With contraception, however, there is no development whatsoever. All Christians opposed it till 1930, then the Anglicans "woke up," and virtually all other Christians have since followed suit. A sheer reversal of a belief is not a "development," by any stretch of the imagination. Why is that not at least as troubling to non-Catholics as, say, the definition of the Assumption of Mary in 1950? The great Anglican apologist C.S. Lewis wrote:

> As regards contraceptives, there is a paradoxical, negative sense in which all possible future generations are the patients or subjects of a power wielded by those already alive. By contraception simply, they are denied existence; by contraception used as a means of selective breeding, they are, without their concurring voice, made to be what one generation, for its own reasons, may choose to prefer. From this point of view, what we call Man's power over Nature turns out to be a power exercised by some men over other men with Nature as its instrument.
>
> (*The Abolition of Man*, New York: Macmillan, 1947, 68-69)

Such change simply can't happen in the Church (see 1 Corinthians 11:2; 2 Thessalonians 2:15; 3:6; 1 Timothy 3:15; Jude 3). To be sure, new technology raises new particular issues and moral dilemmas, but the principles from which we formulate our opinions cannot change because the Moral Law itself does not change.

Birth control does not equal contraception. This is what our society today cannot "see." We Catholics interpret the "contra" part of "contraception" very literally. We believe it is anti-child, anti-conception, anti-procreative purpose of marriage and sexual relations, anti-nature, in a harmful and sinful way. We must recognize crucial distinctions.

NFP, on the other hand, does not violate the natural order, because if the woman is fertile, and the couple wishes to avoid having another child (for the "grave motives" Paul VI referred to, not frivolous, materialistic, or humanistic ones), that couple respects the natural order of things (and each other) and abstains.

There is a real, legitimate, non-trivial, moral, philosophical and ethical distinction between contraception and NFP. Contraception has been compared to Roman vomitoriums. This is a more or less perfect analogy, for what do we think of a person who eats merely for the pleasure of it, and disregards nutrition (bulimia, vomitoriums, junk food junkies, etc.)? Likewise, how do we regard a person who goes to the other extreme, and eats for nutrition, with disdain for the pleasure (extreme health food nuts, Scrooge-types)?

We intuitively sense a perversion of the natural order and of a rational approach to food and life in general. God gave us taste buds; he also ordered food as a necessary agent of bodily (and even psychological) health. We might call the two elements Function and Feeling . . .

Yet when it comes to sex, we wish to separate the two functions with impunity and utter disregard for the personal and societal consequences. Some Puritans, Victorians, and certain types of truly "repressed" Catholics and certain types of fundamentalist Protestants throughout history have minimized or denigrated the pleasure of sex, thinking it a "dirty," "shameful" thing, apart from it's procreative purpose. Some couples never even saw each other unclothed.

This was absurd and wrong, but of course, that is not our problem at all today. Now we have sex at will with no willingness to procreate at all, in many cases. We wink at this perversion, as long as it is confined to marriage. But this profoundly misunderstands the very purpose of marriage.

As soon as God made Eve (and hence began marriage), He told them to "be fruitful and multiply" (Genesis 1:28). Luckily for the human race, Adam and Eve weren't feminists or "progressives" who decided not to have children. These things used to be utterly self-evident, but they are no more. We also find the unitive element, suggested in Genesis 2:18,24-25 (cf. Song of Solomon). This is Catholic teaching: we freely and joyfully acknowledge both aspects.

All we are saying is that they shouldn't be separated in ways which violate the natural order of nature. Nothing in Catholic teaching forbids sex at times when it is determined that the woman is infertile, or in the case of a post-menopausal woman, or one who cannot bear children at all, or a sterile man. That's fine, because it doesn't involve a deliberate decision to ignore fertility and frustrate its natural course.

Contraception fosters and promotes many other sins:

1. It undermines marital fidelity and monogamy by making it easy to commit adultery without the "shameful" consequences of possible offspring.

2. It promotes divorce by making more possible the promiscuity that undermines stable lifelong marriages in the first place. Fear of pregnancy and the societal stigmas that used to be attached to illegitimacy was previously sufficient motive to prevent much infidelity.

3. Likewise, cohabitation is "encouraged" by making "convenient," "consequence-less" fornication possible. If such couples faced the possibility of children, they would be far less likely to live together and fornicate. But as it is, we have both artificial contraceptive methods and abortion -- both perfectly legal and societally encouraged! What a wonderful world for the playboy and "(sexually) liberated woman" to inhabit . . .

4. Homosexuality is similar to the contraceptive mentality, in that, by its very nature, it is non-

reproductive. It is sex for pure pleasure and selfish motives, and an "alternate lifestyle," just as being married with no children, or being in serial "marriages" are "alternate lifestyles" these days. What all these views have in common are their un-Christian and untraditional (and immoral) nature.

5. Abortion is clearly linked to contraception. Apart from what I have already noted above, the "diabolical logic" works (in a hypothetical average pro-abortion woman today) like this:

> A) "I can control my own body and whether I conceive or not, according to my own whims and fancies."
>
> B) "I must fornicate, as it is too strong of a desire to suppress, and why do that, anyway, as it is natural?"
>
> C) "Whether God desires for me to conceive or not is irrelevant, as I am the captain of my own destiny."
>
> D) "If I don't want a child [for whatever reason], I can prevent that by various chemical or 'mechanical' means. Abstention is too difficult, if not impossible, so that is not an option."
>
> E) "I think it would be a 'bad' thing for me to bring a child into the world at this time."
>
> F) [often]: "The world is overpopulated as it is."
>
> G) "If I become pregnant, that was not my will and was a 'mistake'."

II) "I can abort such a 'mistake' because it is my body and I have the right to do with it whatever I please, according to the reasons above. I tried to prevent this conception, but that didn't work, so I will exercise my legal option of abortion, to achieve the same end: no child. It's not yet a child anyway; it feels no pain; it's just a blob of tissue; I'm too young; what will my parents say?" [etc.]

This is the mentality of a typical, non-religious or nominally religious person. Abortion is legal, therefore right and moral; it is a back-up for the Pill, when the Pill fails, etc. No one is happy to abort, and so forth . . . Most evangelical and committed, conservative Orthodox and Catholic and Anglican Christians do far better, as they are taught that abortion is evil (to more or less extents), but most except Catholics have been taken in by the very pagan and humanist philosophy which made widespread abortion possible and actual in the first place.

It is very clear, especially once it is pondered and thought-through, and when all the facts are in. But our society just can't "see" it. It doesn't *want* to see it. And the churches which have caved and compromised with the spirit of the age are at the forefront (by means of their sanction and legitimizing function) of the worldwide return to paganism and pagan sexual practices and attitudes. It is difficult to miss the connection between contraception and the sexual / abortion revolution which it was instrumental in producing, and which couldn't have happened without it.

Thus, the "preventive wisdom" of traditional Christianity in this regard (continued only by Catholicism and some small Protestant sects and Orthodox jurisdictions) is made manifest today beyond all refutation. As always, God knew what He was doing, and He has spoken unambiguously through His Word and through His Church, and via the Vicar of Christ, heroically, in 1968, at the very height of the Revolution and rebellion against tradition and Christianity. We ignore the warnings and spiritual wisdom and sound moral theology, backed up by the events of history and rise and fall of empires, at our own peril.

I do grant that there are real subtleties to the discussion, and that it requires deep ethical and spiritual reflection. In the final analysis, however, I think the best way to describe the widespread reluctance or inability to even understand, let alone adopt NFP and acknowledge the wrongness of contraception, is because modern man simply cannot *hear* these things any more. It is not necessarily a matter of obstinacy or ill will; rather, I would suspect that we have been so inoculated with the "contraceptive mentality" for 70-odd years, that our whole structure of plausibility -- in the West, particularly -- has been transformed. One therefore needs to undergo a "paradigm shift," to borrow a phrase from social psychology.

Both reason and an understanding of Church history are necessary in order to fully grasp what the Catholic Church teaches about NFP and contraception. I should think that the knowledge that all Christians opposed contraception until 1930 would be sufficient to give any conscientious Christian serious pause.

The evil of contraception lies in the "contralife will," and that is primarily exercised (in a practical sense) by frustrating the natural state of things during fertile periods. It doesn't follow that artificial contraception becomes moral during infertile times, because it is intrinsically a grave sin; contrary to the nature of things and the natural law (as Catholics would say homosexual acts also are).

Having sex during non-fertile times in the context of NFP involves no frustration of nature or natural law, but rather it is acting "naturally within nature," when nature happens to be such that no conception will take place. The Catholic Church has never said that a couple can't do that. If that were true, then couples would have to abstain after the woman's menopause, or always, if she were infertile (or if the man had a low sperm count). But that has never been a Church teaching. NFP (rightly understood and practiced) does not entail a contralife will. It is essentially different, though the method can be abused and used in a contraceptive fashion, for the wrong motives.

We don't eat purely for pleasure, or purely for health reasons, to the exclusion of good taste. If someone does that, we think they are weird, because "it is unnatural." We don't go around sticking our elbows in someone's nose, or our toe in their ear. We instinctively know this is strange and unnatural behavior. Likewise, we don't use balloons and rubber cups and pills which mess around with the natural functions of the female reproductive system, in relation to something as sacred and beautiful as moral sex, within marriage. Christians used to instinctively know this, too, but we have bought into the Planned Parenthood / Overpopulation / Children are a Burden pagan mentality.

Couples who practice NFP, in accordance with traditional Catholic teaching on sexuality, abstain, no matter how they feel, during fertile periods. Such is the discipline of a virtuous life, where the assumption of the "freedom of unlimited sex at all times" is denied. This is what has been called "marital chastity." It is not always easy. No one ever said it was. But the good thing is that it actually helps to keep the "spark" in marriage, by simulating the "waiting" and the drama and tension which was present before marriage (in those who didn't sin by fornicating). If they don't have a legitimate reason, then they ought to have sex whenever they like, enjoy it (without having to adhere to the disciplinary "strictness" of NFP), and joyfully accept any child that is conceived.

It is permissible, in Catholic teaching, to limit children, for sufficiently serious reasons. A desire for an extravagant, materialistic, narcissistic, self-centered lifestyle, for example, is not one of these sufficient reasons. To have sex with no intention of ever having children, who are regarded as a "hindrance" and a "burden" and an "inconvenience" is wicked. Sex is supposed to be essentially an act of giving oneself totally to another, within the context of total commitment and love, not "taking" and "abusing" the other solely for lustful or "conquest" purposes. As such it is natural that it produces children, where the love of the couple can be expressed also outward to others who came from them, as a result of their love and unity.

This the essence of things, and the "ontology of sexuality." Breaking down this natural state in fact leads to the horrors of abortion and the appalling lack of respect for life that we see today. If a couple feels that they can thwart a possible conception, then they can -- by a diabolical logical progression – come to regard an unplanned conception as unwanted, therefore able to be killed, by the same reasoning which concludes that they "own their own bodies," rather than being stewards of God's gift, as the Christian view holds. The same reasoning applies to "assisted suicide."

One often hears arguments against the Catholic position which are built upon the false assumption that Catholics supposedly teach (by logical implication) that one must always have sex during fertile periods, or have as many kids as they possibly can (leaving it completely up to nature, etc.), or that all sex must be literally procreative.

This is false. Rather, it is a matter of accepting nature as it is and being "open" in spirit to a new life which might result (rather than being deliberately hostile to it, or being willing to exterminate a precious child as an "inconvenience"). The evil lies in attempting to "mess with nature." Therefore, it is not "anti-procreation" to have sex during infertile times because procreation isn't an issue then. We aren't saying that it is wrong to have sex unless procreation is possible; rather, we are saying that it is wrong to make pleasure an *end in itself*, or the other person the *means to an end* (purely selfish pleasure), or to separate the procreative and unitive purposes for this evil goal by a deliberate act of the will.

Why God made the female reproductive system and menstrual cycle as it is might have any number of possible (but speculative) explanations. Scientists used to think that the appendix had no function, then they figured out that it did. There is a reason for everything in nature. We didn't have a clue about DNA or sub-atomic particles or black holes 150 years ago. Why is a woman pregnant for nine months instead of one? Why can't the child be born at one month gestation so it wouldn't hurt as much, then grow rapidly once born (maybe in a pouch, like a kangaroo)? For that matter, God could have made men and women so that they only desired to have sex with exclusively decent, loyal, committed people, or after they were married, or only till the age of 25, etc.

We can't answer any of these questions with finality, as to why God did or didn't do this, that, or the other. But we can accept reality and the universe as it is; including the moral laws and the consequences of violating them: things we see all around us, so that we no longer have the excuse of ignorance.

The bottom line for a Catholic is whether or not they are willing to accept the authority of the Church on this matter (and it is infallible) and render assent whether or not they fully understand it. It is good to understand as much as we can (and that is my purpose in this very book), but we all have to accept things we don't understand in many areas of life. In this instance, it is a matter of authority and what Christ intended for His Church, and its "claim" over the lives of His followers.

The direction of society is clear: the culture of death and almost unlimited narcissism and hedonism. The dire predictions of *Humanae Vitae* have all come true. Each individual must make a choice between traditional Christian morality or "modern," so-called "progressive and enlightened" ultimately humanist morality.

The problem today is that few people reflect sufficiently on these issues (if at all) to even understand the choice, or know that such a choice exists (let alone substantiated by history and sociology). Such is the completeness of the effect of the sexual revolution on the minds and hearts of anyone in Western Civilization who doesn't make a deliberate, conscious choice to follow a different path: specifically the now (ironically) radically nonconformist option of traditional Christianity.

Chapter Three

Extramarital Sex

The difference between the prevailing secular cultural view of sexuality and the traditional Christian (and particularly, Catholic) perspective lies in the deepest *purpose* of sexuality, which is one of God's greatest gifts. Sex is not *merely* a physical pleasure (like wine, roller coasters, hot tubs, listening to the Beatles or Beethoven, etc.) -- though (praise be to God) moral sex *does* include that as part of its essence; what we call the "unitive" purpose.

Contrary to popular mythology – sadly encouraged by many Christians who possess an insufficient understanding of the theology of the body and the wide-ranging implications of the Incarnation -- God *likes* physical pleasure and the senses. After all, He gave us taste buds (biologically unnecessary) and nerve endings (which make sex enjoyable in the purely physical sense).

Our eyes appreciate aesthetic beauty and our ears beautiful, harmonious music and things like children's laughter and the sound of the mourning dove or waves crashing on the beach. Our noses give us the pleasure of the aroma of fresh-baked bread or a Scotch pine Christmas tree, etc.

It is not, therefore, simply an anti-pleasure motive which causes Christianity to regard extramarital sex as a sin, and therefore to prohibit it (though some truncated brands of Christianity have distorted this concept and wrongly frowned upon pleasure *qua* pleasure).

Sex is a deeply mystical, metaphysical thing, and designed by God to be so. To have sex with a person is to literally become "one flesh" with them (Matthew 19:5-6, 1 Corinthians 6:12-20) -- not just physically, but "mystically" and spiritually as well. So sex profoundly unifies people. Wine and opera don't do that (except in a purely superficial sense). There is an ontological transformation that takes place when intercourse occurs.

People know this. It doesn't take a rocket scientist to understand it. Nor does one have to be a Christian to comprehend this, because we are all human beings made in God's image, and He *designed* sexuality. And we know how it feels (again, not just sensually, but on the *inside*, in our soul and spirit) and how it affects people after it happens.

It is a very strong emotional bond -- as all know who have experienced it. For this reason, orthodox Christianity has always held that sex outside the marital commitment is sinful and wrong, because it is (when all is said and done, and in *essence*, if not always in deliberate *intent*) an *exploitation* of the other for the sake of pleasure. It assumes a physical oneness before the appropriate complete spiritual oneness of life that occurs in properly committed marriage. It's (literally) putting the cart before the horse.

The denial of this has led to a host of problems: divorce, child and spousal abuse, one-parent families, rampant sexually-transmitted disease, and all the mental and emotional agonies resulting from broken relationships.

The sexual revolution has been an abysmal failure, as all honest observers (pro or con) must agree. Free sex without restraint or commitment only hurts people and destroys lives -- especially those of women and children. We are not just animals. We were made to love each other as whole, entire people, as far more than just bodies or convenient body parts.

How could anyone fail to note this, after all that has gone on in the last 40 years? Does anyone seriously contend anymore that we are a *happier* society because we threw off our "Puritanical" restrictions on sexual expression?

Therefore, it is not "love" which urges one to proceed to sex before commitment to the whole person for life. Even our natural instincts tell us that the two ought to go together. Christianity has it exactly right. Protestant apologist C.S. Lewis, in his marvelous book, *The Four Loves*, wrote about how people in love instinctively start talking about being together forever, loving only each other, how the desired is the greatest, most fabulous person in the world, etc. They know *instinctively* -- apart from any necessary Christian moral theology -- that commitment goes hand-in-hand with erotic desires and fulfillments.

Otherwise, it just doesn't work. Not to be overly blunt, but apart from this commitment the woman is reduced to (conservative Jewish talk-show host and psychologist Dr. Laura Schlesinger's term) an "unpaid prostitute." The man likewise becomes a mere object for pleasure. Feminists of all people (even the more radical feminists) should immediately see how premarital sex -- far from being "liberating" for the woman -- promotes and positively *encourages* all the age-old unmarried male exploitations, manipulative sexual/romantic games, and perceptions of women as primarily sexual objects.

The truly "strong woman" whose self-image is properly grounded in God and Christian (even natural law) morality, resists all that, knowing that her sexual allure and feminine appeal to a man is the greatest power she has to "pressure" the man into committing himself to her for a lifetime (by resisting his advances before such commitment). That's just the way it is.

And if one can't trust a future mate (particularly a man) to be strong and to resist sexual temptation before marriage (proven by chastity in the dating relationship), how can one trust them *after* the wedding -- when even greater temptations present themselves, and where it takes a great deal of effort to keep the "flame" going?

The non-Christian notion of marriage and co-habitation is a ticking time-bomb, and offers little emotional security or stability, especially for women. The free-sex "ethos" inevitably punishes women, whereas unscrupulous playboys and philandering types of men can engage in their abuses with the least consequence (though assuredly not without none -- they are not happy in the long run, either).

George Gilder wrote very perceptively about the societal disaster of sexual liberalism in his book, *Men and Marriage*. He noted that the "losers" in the sexual revolution are younger men and older women. Young men have less money and older women have less sexual allure. So, for example, unscrupulous older men can attract younger women with their "power and money," and divorce their wives. But eventually, all are losers who engage in what Christian theology calls "fornication" and "adultery."

The traditional Christian view detests all these sins as abominations – and because they are intrinsically wrong, they destroy lives and do not (in the long run) lead to any sort of self-fulfillment or happiness. This is why we have marital vows. Marriage is much more than just sex and physical gratification. And sex is far more than just physical pleasure, too.

The other thing that should be prominently noted is that procreation is ultimately the primary purpose of sex. This is how we get new people in the world! This was always a "given" until recently, when new philosophies and a prominent cultural hedonism and selfism sought to disconnect sex from producing children, and to make it an end in itself.

And what flows from that? Contraceptive devices and pills led in fact to free sex without responsibility (exemplified at Woodstock and Haight-Ashbury and seemingly one and all TV sitcoms today), leading to further exploitation and misery on a massive scale.

Sex was regarded as an end in itself; therefore people became mere objects, used to fulfill the first end and desire. If a child was created inadvertently (thus regarded as truly an "accident" -- God help us), then society created the "right" to barbarically kill the defenseless child and dispose of the consequences. This "right" now extends even to full-term babies, who (with full legality in the U.S.) have their necks pierced and brains sucked out upon partial emergence from the birth canal so as to not interfere with any "born" persons' "freedoms."

So free sex has been placed on a higher level even than the precious, sacred life of a new human being. This is diabolical and wicked. Free sex inexorably leads to millions of dead, broken preborn children's bodies lying in a heap -- victims of hedonism, materialism, feminism, and expedience. We willingly sacrifice our children to our idol-gods. Child-killing is well-nigh the *sacrament* of radical feminism.

We see, then, how what may appear a simple, harmless thing at first (physical intimacy) leads to massive negative societal consequences, up to and including assembly-line, profiteering murder of innocent "by-products" of such "innocent, loving" activities. To those who claim that free sex is simply "expressing and showing love," I reply that it is not very loving to kill another (tiny) human being (which is the almost-inevitable societal *consequence* of the free love ethic).

To love does not equate with being reduced to an animal. Following this logic, men should try to make love to every good-looking woman they see, on the grounds that refusing to do so would be a lack of love. This wouldn't *necessarily* result from secularistic premises, but it is not *inconsistent* with them. Hedonism and unbridled lust are not Christianity.

If indeed we were *just* animals, then sex would be solely a matter of biology and barnyard antics. Rape wouldn't even be able to be condemned (after all, male animals often force sex upon the females). Marriage would be a purely optional convention, disconnected entirely from any necessary connection to sex.

But few even of the self-proclaimed playboys would take it that far. Try as they may, they can't cast off entirely natural law and God's image in themselves. They are not animals (though they may be much more like them in certain behaviors than a practicing Christian would be).

Clearly, sex means much more between a man and a woman than it does between two hogs or giraffes. We feel a beautiful oneness; we feel like we have opened up the most intimate aspects of ourselves to another human being -- and are therefore made quite vulnerable (the stakes are very high: it's either "heaven" or "hell" at that point). For precisely that reason, God designed sex to be appropriate and entirely good and positive and safe only within the context of a lifelong marital bond and commitment.

All recent sociological experience bears this out. The Christian has far more to appeal to for his case than the Bible or papal proclamations. False moralities always refute themselves in their disastrous historical results. We are living through one such period.

Even secular surveys of married couples and their enjoyment of sex consistently show that Christian couples (especially those who were virgins until they were married) experience a significantly higher level of pleasure in sex than those who are non-Christians, or who have "experimented" before marrying. The truth is exactly the opposite of the cultural myths promulgated by those who have a stake in the promulgation of the sexual revolution. Traditional, orthodox Christians – constantly pilloried as being supposedly against sex -- are in fact enjoying it qualitatively and quantitatively much more than their "liberated, free" counterparts.

That is the quite-ironic truth, but it is sad that so many adopt these secularist, feminist, post-Christian falsehoods, thus dooming themselves to almost certain misery. Sometimes it takes a lot for people to wake up to moral sanity -- even the collapse of an entire civilization.

Purveyors of so-called "liberated" sexuality claim that the Christian view eliminates all the "excitement and romance" of sex. But why can't the *wedding night* contain all this glorious romance and excitement, as it used to? Why does this have to be before marriage to somehow be so exciting and the "climax" of youth? Sex before marriage is wrong because it unites bodies without the appropriate uniting of souls (that is, lifelong commitment made before God and human witnesses).

Morality is not solely determined by good intentions and the absence of force or malice, etc. There are also absolute moral rules which have been time-tested and which are clearly taught in Scripture.

Sin has consequences. They may not be immediately evident (in the case of sexual sin), but in the long run and in society they will be. Many people accept – knowingly, consciously or not -- the libertarian or utilitarian myth that we all live to ourselves, and if we don't mean harm to someone, then it is okay to have sex with them. But -- again – that reduces us to animals and assumes falsely that sex is no different than drinking wine or playing basketball. This is a myth. It is simply untrue -- and I think clearly so.

Viewpoints don't develop in a cultural vacuum. We are fish in a sea. We can do our best to reflect and arrive at informed decisions, but we are still in the sea, and it is what it is. Someone wrote that the most dangerous philosophy was the unacknowledged one (in other words, we all have one, conscious or not).

Extramarital sex is *objectively* or *inherently* sinful, which means that its wrongness is not dependent on the attitudes of the ones committing it. Traditional Christians believe it is wrong, on biblical and natural law philosophical grounds, not because of its consequences. My discussion about societal consequences, as outlined above, is based on the following logical argument:

1) we will assume that x is a sin for the sake of argument.

2) then we will examine the consequences of x in the individual and on society, to see if they are harmful or good.

3) we found many harmful consequences.

4) Ergo: though this doesn't prove that x is a sin in and of itself, yet it is consistent with the notion that it is a sin, since we start with the assumption that sins have harmful effects.

Extramarital sex is not necessarily always lustful (nor is marital sex always without lust, because lust is an interior attitude or disposition, where the other person is regarded solely as an object and not as whole person). But it is sinful because it perverts the deepest meaning of sex and objectively exploits the other, whether or not one intends to do so.

The willingness to attain total intimacy of body without the accompanying intimacy of soul and spirit (as exemplified and "proven" by a lifelong commitment) constitutes the refusal to *truly* love (as opposed to the touchy-feely, superficial sort of love promoted by our culture).

Sex outside of marriage, in its deepest meaning, is *not* an act of love, no matter how "good" it feels, no matter how pure and noble the intent is, because it disregards the deepest purpose of sex, which is procreation and spiritual unity, not merely physical pleasure for its own sake (even if it is "in the name of" romantic love).

This is Christian ethics. It may be a tough pill to swallow, but the Christian life is not easy; Jesus never promised us that it would be. If we were only animals, it wouldn't be an issue. We could copulate to our hearts' content, with utter disregard for spirituality or consequences or a universal moral code.

This is traditional Christian teaching, and it is, without a doubt, the clear biblical teaching. Anyone who claims to be a Christian and disciple of Jesus Christ must decide what they will do, with regard to the reality of Christian teaching on sexuality.

Society, however, has obviously chosen a different course. The fruits of free sex are all around us. "The bad tree produces bad fruit" -- said Jesus. In one way or another, the chief debate on these issues always seems to come down to orthodox, traditional Christianity vs. humanism, secularism, atheism, libertarianism, and theological liberalisms.

In many issues Muslims and Orthodox and Conservative Jews would also agree with traditional Protestant, Catholic, and Orthodox teaching on sexuality, perhaps even Buddhists and other eastern religionists. It is, therefore, essentially a battle against secular humanist notions of sexuality and person freedom that the Christian must wage, personally, and culturally.

The Catholic and traditional Christian definition of sexual freedom is the use of sexuality in the way that God intended it to be used (based on His revelation) for the greatest fulfillment of human beings. He created it, and is omniscient, so He knows how it is best and most properly used. Immoral use of sex is not "freedom" but bondage. It is possible also to reformulate this definition in a "theologically-free," secular fashion:

> Sexual freedom is that use of sexuality which proves in the long run to work out best for the purposes of human happiness and fulfillment: emotionally, mentally, and physically, and which produces the most stability in families/relationships and hence in society, minimizing broken homes, heartbreak, disease, dysfunctional relationships, spousal and child abuse, rape, sexual harassment, etc. Avoidance of these ill results can be a working definition of "happiness and fulfillment" for our purposes. Long-term effects of various sexual lifestyles are determined by scientific sociological studies of same.

In my view, the two formulations are ultimately one and the same. I contend that that which can be shown to be best for human beings in the above sense is identical to traditional Christian morality. We have the advantage now of hindsight regarding the abysmal societal results of 40 years of wild sexual experimentation and radicalism.

The second formulation is secular (almost utilitarian), not involving any peculiarly religious concepts. If the second definition can be shown to be true, and the successful lifestyles are essentially the same as traditional Christian ones, then my religious definition has been strongly supported.

I think this has, in fact, already been established by the history of the last forty years and many existing scientific studies, such as those involving the effects of divorce on children, the negative effects of co-habitation, effects of constant day-care, the link of breast cancer, infertility, and other problems to abortion and contraceptive techniques, the subsequent marital histories of promiscuous persons, the link of crime and drugs to (in addition to poverty) broken homes: particularly those lacking a father for young boys, and so forth. This is a very important discussion on many levels (personal, societal, ethical, philosophical).

One way of approaching discussions of normative sexuality, and particularly Christian morality, is the utilization of what I call the "reverse pragmatic argument": "if something is true it *in fact* works" (as opposed to straight pragmatism: "something is true *because* it works"). One mustn't separate "freedom" from responsibility in matters moral (let alone sexual). Otherwise, one would have to assert that a person ought to be free to engage in "irresponsible sexual conduct" -- and no respectable ethical system would maintain that.

I see several problems with the current societally accepted conception of "sexual freedom" within the relativist, "1960s free love," hedonistic and narcissistic, "if it feels good, do it" framework:

1) Simply equating "freedom" with "choice" does not resolve anything in this particular discussion, since it is not about freedom of choice or will per se, but rather, sexual *ethics*.

2) Once the spectre of "choice" comes up one must immediately ask, "choice to do *what*?" That brings the discussion back to a consideration of the relative merits of different views of sexuality based on the agreed-upon criteria of "goodness" or "badness" -- in turn based on the ill (or good) results potentially or actually produced by said views.

3) That in turn leads to the inevitable question of what (sexually) *is* wrong, improper, unnatural, or however one wishes to categorize these things. This is unavoidable, because virtually all people in fact agree (I believe) that certain sexual practices are wrong or harmful (rape, clitorectomies, manipulation of people for sexual ends, pedophilia, bestiality, sexual harassment in the workplace, child pornography, sexual slavery, publishing of nude photos of someone on the Internet without their permission, rampant promiscuity, etc.).

4) So now the question becomes: "where does one draw the line as to what is proper and improper (or, right or wrong), and on what basis is this done?" Simply asserting "I am free to do whatever I please and this is sexual freedom" is far more a statement about license, hedonism or libertinism than it is about sexual ethics. Everyone would place *some* limits on sexual behavior.

5) Even the results of various lifestyles -- if they are to be observed on any objective plane whatever -- must be "judged"

based on the facts and scientific studies, whereby we can determine if they actually produced the "human happiness and fulfillment" which everyone desires. Simply believing or wishing that this be the case is not enough. All that proves is that someone wants to be happy within a certain parameter of sexual choices; it proves nothing at all about whether those choices will, in fact, make them happy in the long run.

6) This is one of the basic fallacies of libertarianism. It is tacitly assumed that whatever a person *thinks* will make them happy (for example, heroin or the playboy lifestyle or excessive materialism) will *in fact* do so. The long-term consequences for both the individual and the society are rarely taken into account. There is also the myth of the atomistic individual, as if individual choices and courses of action can be made in an airtight bubble, without affecting others around them. It is all about freedom and hardly at all about responsibility and foreseen possible consequences. But that is the *zeitgeist* of our times, sadly enough.

7) Individualism is the watchword; community and social cohesiveness and commonality are largely ignored. One could argue that this has been an increasing trend since the Renaissance, actually, excepting those portions of society which consciously rejected this extreme individualistic autonomy for some communitarian vision. Christianity is unabashedly communitarian, though its adherents are practically as susceptible as everyone else to succumbing to the temptation of prevailing cultural forces and fashionable ideas.

We can only go by large-scale societal results of these beliefs and practices. Individual exceptions of self-reported "happiness and fulfillment" can always be produced, but they are merely "anecdotal" and of little importance statistically. What objective basis does the advocate of the sexual revolution and rejection of Christian sexual ethics produce, apart from the mere wish or "prediction" that such a choice will bring happiness?

Certainly the ones on the cutting edge of such "brave new choices" (the Hollywood elite, the arts and music communities, academia, etc.) are not sterling examples of happiness, as a result of their rejection of traditional Christian sexual morality. I see much misery and brokenness; not much true happiness and fulfillment.

The sociological data shows that, for example, statistically, those who live together are far less likely to attain to a successful, happy marriage than those who waited and (especially) who have a strong faith. The happiest, most sexually satisfied marriages, generally-speaking, are those of committed Christians who waited till they got married.

The determination of Mr./Miss Wrong or Mr./Miss Right is far more effectively and accurately made without the rose-colored glasses of sexual involvement being in the way. How good someone is in bed does not give one iota of information as to how good a marriage partner they might be. Two hogs or walruses can copulate (and enjoy it). What does that prove?: exactly nothing. Families and marriages in our culture are falling apart all around us. They were not doing that at nearly the same rate forty years ago.

One must attempt to explain why that is. I say it is the new "liberated" sexual ethic that is the primary causative factor. The damage has been done: usually to children, who are the greatest victims of all this sexual nonsense and extreme narcissism and hedonism that has gone on since the sexual revolution.

What are "healthy sexual feelings," and how does one determine such a thing? Most people would, I presume, tell a 60-year-old man who had sodomized 40 young boys that he was acting in quite an "unhealthy" fashion (if not much more). I draw the line or "immoral sex" in a different place than most secularists or social liberals or libertarians would, but, assuredly, we all draw lines and say "x is wrong." But how do we decide on a secularist basis where these "lines" ought to be drawn?

One must go back to the nature and purpose of sex and sexual organs to really examine this issue. It is a question of drawing the line again. Most persons would agree that sex between a man and a cow or a rhinoceros is wrong, or "unnatural," if that terminology is preferred. Christians think sex between two men or two women or unmarried heterosexual men and women is wrong, too. The line of what is considered "natural" is simply drawn in a different place.

What is fascinating to discuss (in a philosophical or ethical vein) is why people draw the lines where they do: their justifications for doing so, beyond the usual "it feels good" or "I can't help it." The Christian/Muslim/traditional Jewish view (if I may digress a moment and become necessarily graphic) is very straightforward and simple: Penises were designed for vaginas, not anuses. This is anatomically, visually, and biologically obvious.

Sexual organs were designed primarily for reproductive purposes. Therefore, to totally deny that purpose and to use them for pleasure only is to engage in fundamentally unnatural acts. Even if one takes the potentially theistic notion of "design" out of the equation, one can still construct the argument based on biology and natural selection and on a health basis. The view can be fleshed out with great complexity, sophistication, and nuance (and theologically) but that is the fundamental notion, bottom-line.

The usual libertarian mistake and fallacy is to not see the connection between individual choices and societal fallout. Sexual liberals don't seem to acknowledge that these "particulars" of people's sex life are *precisely* what pave the way for massive societal and familial upheaval. Otherwise, what has caused these things? If I am told that poverty is the main culprit, I reply that families were pretty strong during the Great Depression, and that African-Americans now have more money than they have ever had, yet their families are falling apart.

If I am told that hedonism and recklessness are distortions of what is proposed by non-Christians to be "sexual freedom," I have to be shown how the two views cannot in any way be causally connected to each other (which gets into "slippery slope" scenarios). I submit that it can't be done.

Catholicism, and Christianity, generally-speaking, is not "anti-sex." It simply places limits on what is proper sexuality, just as everyone else does, at one place or another. Christianity is against sex with no limits or boundaries whatever, but so are most other people. We are simply more restrictive. Any restriction on sexuality is seen as "oppressive" by a society which thinks that no one can possibly live without sex, and a lot of it.

The only way to have a constructive discussion on sex is to go back to the premises behind each position, not simply bringing up hellish "hard-case" scenarios intended to make the Christian position look ridiculous and unworkable, when it is not at all. No progress is made, then, because none of the underlying assumptions of either position are properly dealt with, so that both sides can understand why the other takes the position that it does.

Christians oppose filth and vulgarity in the public arena. One can argue till the cows come home about what those are, of course, but there is such a concept as opposing them without adopting silly, stupid, and shallow (and unbiblical) Puritanistic, Victorian moralism and prudery, or putting underwear on Michelangelo's *David* or a bra on the *Venus de Milo*. One need not choose between the two extremes. There are other more sensible Christian positions.

The trouble is, these discussions tend to immediately become "politicized" and "polemicized" and any position other than one's own caricatured, mocked, and dismissed. The Christian position on this is not at all as simple as people are making out. The biblical, Christian (Catholic) view is not identical to that taken by the 1st Fundamentalist Storefront Church in Podunk, where the women have to wear ankle-length dresses and the men can't have any facial hair; and where wine, dancing, and rock music are intrinsically wicked.

Often, reactions to Christian pronouncements on immoral sex are mere emotionalism and people being angry about various events in their personal past or our recent cultural past, which they associate with (various forms of) Christianity, rightly or wrongly, so that Christians become a target as so-called "representatives" of some "Christian" position, and recipient of all the pent-up aggravation and indignation.

In public schools and in the media for the last 30 years or so, children got one monolithic view: free sex with no (or very few) restrictions; (Christian) restrictions are oppressive remnants of the Inquisition, Victorian era, and so forth. After the resultant chaos now things are starting to balance out a bit. It is unutterably tragic, however, that many millions of lives had to suffer greatly in the interim from yet another Grand Social Experiment and deliberate rejection of traditional Christian morality.

There are all kinds of versions of Christianity and just as many distortions of biblical/Christian teaching (especially in application to real-world situations). And there are Christian parents who don't have a clue as to how to raise Christian disciples rather than clone-like automatons who grow up with all the "right" and "correct" liberal and secular ideas. If Christian parents do not make sure that their children receive a Christian education, in addition to a secular one, they are basically yielding them up to secularism and the current relativistic, narcissistic *zeitgeist*. That being the case, we would expect these Christian kids to be little different from their friends around them. Peer pressure is extremely influential. They will receive all the usual fashionable ideas, ethical, sexual, and otherwise, by osmosis.

People often ask -- in a related vein -- about a traditional Christian view of dating. Proper "Christian dating" would not include sex: not all of it, at any rate. Limited expressions of "semi-sexual" affection (if there is such a thing -- our sexual nature and how much sex is a part of ourselves on a very deep level is a very complex discussion) are recognized and accepted in most traditional Christian views on the matter, excepting the ultra-strict ones.

The usual Christian understanding would be that foreplay and similar acts of expression which arouse sexual desire were intended and designed by God (or biology, in a secular sense) to be precursors of intercourse, so one must be vigilant in knowing how far they can go before the arousal takes over and their will starts to yield to passion.

It seems altogether sensible to do everything possible to avoid falling in love with anyone unless there is a reasonable assurance that the other would make a halfway decent marital partner. Romantic love itself communicates this thought to us. Once romantic love arrives, what do couples invariably say?: "I want to be with you *forever*." So the Christian view merely recognizes that inherent, natural need in human beings and attempts to place sex and erotic love within the safest confines of the committed, permanent marital relationship, where the couple makes a vow before God and the community to be faithful to each other.

It's difficult enough even then, because people are people, and we are all sinners, with many selfish tendencies that mitigate against "outward-love." But this is the best way to protect the love and acceptance and lasting intimacy we all crave and desire.

Many sexual liberals seem to think that people who abstain until marriage know less about each other (in order to make an informed choice) than those who dash right to sex on the first (or third) date, putting the cart before the horse. But most people of any belief would instinctively recognize, I think (or know from personal experience), how sexual infatuation blinds one's judgment. Romantic love can, too, but adding sex into the equation makes it far worse and far more dangerous, as to long-term consequences.

Good, emotionally fulfilling, personally rewarding sex ultimately flows from a true, committed love of the whole person, and the desire to please *them* out of gratitude for who they are, not from just their sexual prowess or attractive body parts. It doesn't flow from the more practice one gets doing it. That's what the "sexually-liberated" person doesn't appear to "get" anymore.

Sex is not primarily about the "plumbing" or the technique. It is about two people who love each other who happen to also have the right plumbing, which works excellently when all the other pieces of the puzzle of human marital relationships are properly in place. The "hot water heater" of sexual passion (forgive my ridiculous analogy) is the commitment of the partners, not expertise gained from pop sex books or all the psychobabble that passes for knowledge these days.

Unfortunately, far too many Christians (probably a majority, sadly) have not understood even the truly Christian conception of sexuality and its purpose. There are often abuses in Christian contexts. Christians are human beings, and sexual beings. If their needs aren't met, they start looking elsewhere, rather than seek the deeper causes and roots of their problems and staying faithful to their marriage vows. And invariably, the children suffer through all this human folly and wrongdoing.

Certain strains of a Christian fundamentalism which borders on Gnosticism in its disdain of pleasure and matter, have obviously never become familiar with the Song of Solomon:

> Your two breasts are like two fawns, twins of a gazelle . . .
>
> Your lips distil nectar, my bride; honey and milk are under your tongue; the scent of your garments is like the scent of Lebanon.
>
> . . . Let my beloved come to his garden, and eat its choicest fruits.
>
> I come to my garden, my sister, my bride, I gather my myrhh with my spice, I eat my honeycomb with my honey, I drink my wine with my milk.
>
> Eat, O friends, and drink: drink deeply, O lovers!
>
> (4:5; 11; 16; 5:1-2)

I have read that John Milton wrote some extremely sizzling love poetry as well (I'm sure other Christian examples could be found). It's a shame that Christians so often are prudish, when it is not at all a biblical attitude. No doubt the contrast of the pagans and their debaucheries had a lot to do with this, in early Christianity (we see it in the Church Fathers), just as the sexual revolution today has caused an overreaction amongst some Christians. It is a strong human tendency to throw the baby out with the bath water.

I have heard it argued by a thoughtful Christian writer, however, that the sexual revolution can be accounted for in part by the yearning for some sort of mystical experience, once a person has forsaken Christianity or some other religion. Sex fits the bill for an easily accessible, powerful, quasi-mystical or spiritual experience, and that would explain in part why pornography and promiscuity are so rampant in previously quite-Christian countries such as the Netherlands and America.

On the other hand, in areas not previously Christian, such as parts of Africa now experiencing tremendous revival, sexual morals are much higher. Post-Christian countries always have worse morals than countries recently introduced to Christianity. This is true throughout Christian history as well. The "barbarians" such as the Goths and Visigoths usually had higher morals from natural virtues than power-hungry Christian rulers who were trying to convert them, who were visiting prostitutes and engaging in various power schemes. The higher one goes up the ladder of spirituality, the farther the fall if they forsake the climb. Or, as Jesus put it, "to whom much is given, much is required."

Pornography flows from the hedonist impulse and sexual addiction. One seeks after more and more pleasure, thus receiving less and less. Each sexual encounter offers less thrill than the last, so the "spark" is sought in pornography: some sort of variety or titillation previously unknown. Thus hard-core pornography gets worse and worse, violence, pedophilia, bestiality, rape, sadomasochism, etc., so that the all-powerful lust for lustful pleasure can be fulfilled. Once this journey is begun, it has a dynamic all its own, without the remotest relationship to Christianity in its moral dimensions and entire outlook on life, the purpose of sex, and the dignity of women (and men).

It isn't the restriction of sex to marriage that is a problem, but an unhealthy, warped, silly, harmful, prudish approach to sex education. Society ought to encourage an openness and unashamed acceptance of sexuality, but under proper boundaries and parameters where it can be most enjoyable and fulfilling to all parties involved. Pope John Paul II has written much about this. One of his main ongoing projects has been the development of a theology of the body: a much-needed commentary and analysis, and long overdue.

I have often used in my posts the terminology of "traditional Christian morality" or "historical Christian sexual teaching" and so forth. When I do that, I am being precisely accurate, as for most of Christian history, there was an overwhelming consensus on these matters. It is only since the onset of theological liberalism in the last 200 or so years that there have developed 1001 different views. I oppose the myth that these views are somehow exclusively and/or intrinsically Catholic. Things have changed drastically with regard to various tenets of sexual morality in Christian circles.

The historical perspective is supremely important to understand where we got to where we are today in terms of ideas and sexual norms. Many (perhaps most) Christians have simply assimilated the surrounding secular, pagan relativistic and hedonistic sexual ethic (in other words, the relatively unexamined tenets of the sexual revolution). That in itself is no new thing. It has been going on since the beginning of Christianity, which is why periodic revival is so necessary. But the alarming, *widespread nature* of the process today is something relatively rare in Christian history.

It is often charged that the views of the Catholic Church on sexuality are "puritanical" or amount to "prudery." But prudery and being ashamed of the body and sexuality (morally practiced) are entirely different from respecting the natural law and desiring to "be fruitful and [to] multiply." The former is unbiblical and closer in spirit to Gnosticism or Docetism than to Christianity; the latter is quite biblical.

With regard to prudery, attitudes towards nudity, and so forth, the discussion is much more complex (ethically and historically), but I maintain that Victorianism or (what society perceives and defines as) "Puritanism" is a distortion of historic, biblical Christian teaching, which does *not* regard the body and sexuality as evil. That's precisely why the Gnostic and Manichaean heresies were so vigorously opposed by the early Church.

A healthy attitude towards sex, the body, and nudity (in art and so forth) is not the equivalent of the free sexual ethic of the sexual revolution. Nor is it fundamentally non-Christian or unbiblical. As is so often the case with non-Christians looking at Christianity, the critic constructs rigid "either/or" scenarios, so that the choice is "Victorian, Puritanistic, prudish, repressed, Gnostic-influenced Christian" vs. "liberated, uninhibited, psychologically-healthy, fun-loving advocate of free sex." The choices are not at all that stark and simple, within the Christian worldview, even the "traditional" or so-called "backward" Catholic view.

Chapter Four

Divorce

It is often stated that Catholic annulments are simply "Catholic divorce" under another name, as if it is a sort of word play or rationalization on the part of the Catholic Church. And, invariably, it is pointed out that there are many thousands more annulments a year in the United States than there used to be. The higher numbers can be explained in two ways:

> 1) More and more people have not the slightest inkling of what a "sacramental marriage" is, and what responsibilities it entails; hence; these "marriages" were never sacramentally valid (and this is the key) in the first place. This would be a *legitimate* reason for greater numbers.

> 2) Heterodox priests and bishops may be abusing the power to annul marriages; giving in to societal pressure, which would be a grave sin on their part, possibly leading to their damnation if they willfully persist in violating Church teaching. This would be an *illegitimate* reason.

I suspect it is a combination of both factors, because both are major problems in the Catholic Church today. Annulment -- properly understood -- is not divorce at all. Rather, it is the determination that the proper elements of a valid, consummated, sacramental marriage were *never met in the first place*. If a marriage is sacramentally valid, it cannot be annulled by any power on earth. It may appear to be so, but it is not in God's eyes.

Even in civil law, in most countries of the world (especially those with a Christian heritage), a distinction is made between divorce and annulment (see, e.g., *The Oxford Companion to Law*, or *Black's Law Dictionary*).

As to the somewhat complex qualities and characteristics of a valid sacramental marriage (too varied and complex to deal with here), the *Catechism of the Catholic Church* discusses these in its Part II, chapter 3, Article 7; numbers 1601-1666.

The Old Testament distinction between a concubine and a wife is somewhat analogous to the Catholic distinction between civil and sacramental marriage -- itself the kernel and foundational premise of the concept of annulment. Sarah told Abraham to have sexual intercourse with the slave girl Hagar in order to produce a child (because she was barren up till that time).

This was a Hebrew custom in those days. Concubines were protected by Mosaic law (Exodus 21:7-11, Deuteronomy 21:10-14), though they were distinguished from wives (Judges 8:31) and were more easily divorced (Genesis 21:10-14).

God approved of the sending away of Hagar and her son Ishmael (Genesis 21:12), not because they were evil or disparaged by Him (see Genesis 17:20, 21:13,17-20), but because Sarah was Abraham's wife in the fuller sense (akin to sacramental Marriage -- see Gen 17:15-21; cf. Gal 4:21-31).

But later prophets encouraged monogamy (Malachi 2:14 ff.) and the ideal woman of Proverbs 31 lived in a monogamous society. Later, of course, Jesus taught that monogamy (with no divorce) was God's ideal from the beginning (Matthew 19:1-12; cf. Genesis 2:24). Divorce -- so Jesus said – was permitted to the Jews only because of "hardness of heart."

But the "except for fornication" clause of Matthew 19:9 is interpreted by Catholics (and, I believe, the Fathers) as a case of non-matrimonial ongoing fornication as opposed to real marriage, and as such is a biblical basis for annulments, along with the Pauline privilege (1 Corinthians 7:15), which has always been accepted by the Church.

Furthermore, the Old Testament teaches us that there was such a thing as a "strange wife" (KJV), meaning a wife from a foreign land, of a different religion. The result when the Jews married foreigners was often an adoption of their idolatrous worship. This was why God forbade them from marrying such "wives." And this is another example of a "marriage" which really was no marriage; at least not as God intended it to be.

The basic principle was laid out in Deuteronomy 17:17: "Neither shall he multiply wives to himself, that his heart turn not away . . . "; also Deuteronomy 7:3-4: "Neither shalt thou make marriages with them . . . For they will turn away thy son from following me, that they may serve other gods . . . " (KJV). A concrete example is later offered, in the case of King Solomon:

> But king Solomon loved many strange women, together with the daughter of Pharaoh, women of the Moabites, Ammonites, Edomites, Zidonians, and Hittites: Of the nations concerning which the LORD said unto the children of Israel, Ye shall not go in to them, neither shall they come in unto you: for surely they will turn away your heart after their gods: Solomon clave unto these in love. And he had seven hundred wives, princesses, and three hundred concubines: and his wives turned away his heart.
>
> For it came to pass, when Solomon was old, that his wives turned away his heart after other gods: and his heart was not perfect with the LORD his God, as was the heart of David his father. For Solomon went after Ashtoreth the goddess of the Zidonians, and after Milcom the abomination of the Ammonites.
>
> And Solomon did evil in the sight of the LORD, and went not fully after the LORD, as did David his father. Then did Solomon build an high place for Chemosh, the abomination of Moab, in the hill that is before Jerusalem, and for Molech, the abomination of the children of Ammon.

And likewise did he for all his strange wives, which burnt incense and sacrificed unto their gods.

(1 Kings 11:1-8; KJV; cf. Exodus 23:31-33, 34:12-16)

Solomon's unfaithfulness was recounted in the Book of Nehemiah:

Did not Solomon king of Israel sin by these things? . . . even him did outlandish women cause to sin. Shall we then hearken unto you to do all this great evil, to transgress against God in marrying strange wives?

(Nehemiah 13:26-27; KJV; cf. Ezra 9:1-2,14-15)

Lastly, we have a full account of the Israelites sending away these "strange wives" because they never should have married them in the first place, under the Law of God. This is almost exactly analogous to an annulment. The marriages were never "legal" or in accord with God's teaching from the outset:

Now when Ezra had prayed, and when he had confessed, weeping and casting himself down before the house of God, there assembled unto him out of Israel a very great congregation of men and women and children: for the people wept very sore. And Shechaniah the son of Jehiel, one of the sons of Elam, answered and said unto Ezra,

> We have trespassed against our God, and have taken strange wives of the people of the land: yet now there is hope in Israel concerning this thing. Now therefore let us make a covenant with our God to put away all the wives, and such as are born of them, according to the counsel of my lord, and of those that tremble at the commandment of our God; and let it be done according to the law.

> Arise; for this matter belongeth unto thee: we also will be with thee: be of good courage, and do it.

Then arose Ezra, and made the chief priests, the Levites, and all Israel, to swear that they should do according to this word. And they sware. Then Ezra rose up from before the house of God, and went into the chamber of Johanan the son of Eliashib: and when he came thither, he did eat no bread, nor drink water: for he mourned because of the transgression of them that had been carried away.
And they made proclamation throughout Judah and Jerusalem unto all the children of the captivity, that they should gather themselves together unto Jerusalem; And that whosoever would not come within three days, according to the counsel of the princes and the elders, all his substance should be forfeited, and himself separated from the congregation of those that had been carried away. Then all the men of Judah and Benjamin gathered themselves together unto Jerusalem within three days . . . And Ezra the priest stood up, and said unto them,

> Ye have transgressed, and have taken strange wives, to increase the trespass of Israel. Now therefore make confession unto the LORD God of your fathers, and do his pleasure: and separate yourselves from the people of the land, and from the strange wives.

Then all the congregation answered and said with a loud voice,

> As thou hast said, so must we do. But the people are many, and it is a time of much rain, and we are not able to stand without, neither is this a work of one day or two: for we are many that have transgressed in this thing . . .

> And among the sons of the priests there were found that had taken strange wives: namely, of the sons of Jeshua the son of Jozadak, and his brethren; Maaseiah, and Eliezer, and Jarib, and Gedaliah. And they gave their hands that they would put away their wives; and being guilty, they offered a ram of the flock for their trespass . . .
>
> All these had taken strange wives: and some of them had wives by whom they had children.
>
> (Ezra 10:1-13,18-19,44; KJV)

The Old Testament evidence for annulment (by strong analogy), is stronger than for many doctrines that all Christians accept, such as the resurrection of the body, heaven, the atonement of Christ, original sin, the Eucharist, and other doctrines, which were all developed much more fully in the New Testament.

In this case, too, the New Testament builds explicitly upon the kernels of the Old Testament. St. Paul's teaching concerning the departure of the unbeliever (1 Corinthians 7:15 – the "Pauline privilege") hearkens back to this Old Testament teaching, as does his following admonition:

> Do not be mismated [KJV: "unequally yoked] with unbelievers. For what paretnership have righteousness and iniquity. Or what fellowship has light with darkness? What accord has Christ with Belial? Or what has a believer in common with an unbeliever? What agreement has the temple of God with idols? . . .
>
> (2 Corinthians 6:14-16)

Chapter Five

Homosexuality

> . . . God gave them up to dishonorable passions. Their women exchanged natural relations for unnatural, and the men likewise gave up natural relations with women and were consumed with passion for one another, men committing shameless acts with men and receiving in their own persons due penalty for their error.

(Romans 1:26-27)

St. Paul is arguing, then, that there is such a thing as *natural* [sexual] *relations* and its contrary, *unnatural* [sexual] *relations*. He is appealing to natural law and nature: God's created order, and all that that entails. Some things are natural, some are not.

He draws a contrast between natural and unnatural, and also between heterosexual and homosexual sex. Paul is not merely saying that being *consumed with passion* is what is sinful, but the very *concept* and *practice* of homosexual relations, which goes against nature. The documented medical consequences of engaging in such unnatural and unhealthy sexual practices bear this out.

Since it is "unnatural" for men to be (sexually) with men, and women with women, according to the Apostle (and God, since the Bible is God-breathed), he describes the sexual acts as *shameless* and *error*. There is no qualification here for things like rape or promiscuity or uncommitted, manipulative sex (that is the desperate eisegesis of those who already believe the Bible is neutral on the issue).

Sin is always dangerous. God tries to spare us of its consequences, but we are too dense and rebellious to accept Him at His word, and we insist on playing with fire, defying even nature itself, if need be.

Romans 1:18-32 is an argument from nature, a sort of primitive teleological argument (or, argument from design). He implies sins against nature in 1:24: . . . *the dishonoring of their bodies among themselves*. Idolatry is condemned in 1:25: . . . *they . . . worshiped and served the creature rather than the Creator . . .* Immoral sex amounts to a worship of the physical body as an object apart from the whole person who possesses it, and in defiance of the lifelong commitment within which moral sex is protected and placed in the proper context of whole love relationships with whole people (not just genitals), for a whole lifetime.

St. Paul makes a similar argument from nature (but a bit more sophisticated and theological) in 1 Corinthians 6:12-20, by stating that excessive appetite for sex (and also food?) amounts to being *enslaved* (6:12). He exclaims:

> Do you not know that he who joins himself to a prostitute becomes one body with her? For, as it is written, "The two shall become one flesh."

(1 Corinthians 6:16)

In other words, there is an ontological, created reality and natural order beyond mere physical pleasure, which must not be violated. Certain things are wrong by their very nature. Sex outside of marriage -- whether heterosexual or homosexual -- belongs in that category. Paul continues:

> Shun immorality. Every other sin which a man commits is outside the body; but the immoral man sins against his

own body. Do you not know that your body is a temple of the Holy Spirit within you, which you have from God? You are not your own; you were bought with a price. So glorify God in your body.

(1 Corinthians 6:18-20)

So heterosexual fornication and adultery are just as sinful, wicked, reprehensible, and unnatural as homosexual sex. These sexual sins violate the *bounds* of proper sex between males and females as God intended it: within a lifelong monogamous commitment of marriage. The same physical act which is right and proper and beautiful in one situation (in a marriage) becomes sinful in another (with a prostitute, or with one other than one's spouse). Homosexuality also violates this boundary but it goes a step further and violates the created order of sex itself, which God intended for male and female (and I think this is self-evident in the complementary physiology of the reproductive organs, and in the end result of conception).

One might say that fornication is an "ontological" sin against the moral "concept" of marriage, while homosexual sex sins both against the purpose of sex and the ontological, metaphysical, and spiritual (even physical) nature of sex itself.

The next logical step is bestiality. The move has already been made from opposite sex and procreation to same sex and pleasure-only. In so doing, God's laws and natural law are spurned and scorned. So why not make the move to an animal, if the purpose is simply pleasure? Someone may find that distasteful, but utilizing non-Christian logic in sexual matters, no objection can really be made on a non-arbitrary basis.

On the other hand, St. Paul seems to teach that *all* forms of sexual immorality are a sin against nature and against the Holy Spirit within us. Something bad actually happens in the very real spiritual realm. We become joined with the harlot. We sin against ourselves and our own bodies as well. We violate the temple of God (ourselves, if we are Christians, since the Holy Spirit indwells us).

The assertion by radical homosexual exegetes that traditional Christians are distorting the Bible's teaching (whether it is inspired and preserved properly or not) and not presenting it properly, out of alleged nefarious, so-called "homophobic" motives, is groundless. The Bible, as it reads, is indisputably opposed to homosexual acts as a sin against nature, God, and one's own body.

There have always been social stigmas imposed on sinful (or even merely societally harmful) behaviors -- and rightly so. Not long ago illegitimacy was socially stigmatized, on the grounds that childbearing belonged in the context of marriage. Fornication and living together used to be frowned upon. It is right for society to impose "sanctions" of disapproval, so as to enforce its mores and norms.

It isn't right to hate or despise people who have adopted sinful behaviors (Christianity has never taught that, and utterly condemns it), but social stigmas are perfectly normal and natural, and they exist in all societies, because all societies have moral codes that they teach and enforce in one way or another. Thanks be to God that racism is now largely stigmatized. This is a great development in our own lifetimes.

Not long ago, the abortionist was considered the lowest form of murderer, and exploiter of women. Now he is tantamount to a hero in pro-abortionist circles. His profession has been generally despised ever since pagan Greek society produced the Hippocratic Oath some 2200 years ago, but now he has moved up the societal ladder to "equal respect and moral approval" granted to the "child-killing orientation."

After all, the Supreme Court has given what he does total legitimacy, has it not? Admittedly, the court erred by ruling that Dred Scott was property rather than a person back in 1857, but we have progressed much since then . . . now we know that black people are people.

Maybe one day we will become enlightened and "progressive" enough to know that little people are people, too, and not owned by their mothers, and not the proper subjects for being torn limb from limb or having their brains sucked out right before birth (with the approval of Presidents and dozens of senators and congressmen).

Divorce was frowned upon not long ago. In the 1950s (even into the 60s) it was utterly scandalous and embarrassing to say that one's parents were divorced. Now one who initiates a divorce is merely embarking on "personal fulfillment" and "change of lifestyle," etc. Adultery is winked at (I won't recount rather notorious recent examples of well-known public figures).

Euthanasia and assisted suicide were relegated to the morbid and surreal; Nazi-like in their implications not long ago. Now it is law in more and more places, such as in the Netherlands: formerly a stronghold for Calvinist Christianity, and with a heroic record of resistance against the Nazis.

Filthy language, violence, and portrayals of (usually immoral) sex in movies and on television were considered unacceptable not long ago . . . All these things have moved up the ladder to public acceptance. Why not the homosexual lifestyle?

All these examples illustrate that true and right traditions are being broken down in our time, and things are being called good which only a short time ago were considered bad. The last remnants of Christian civilization are being attacked: the nature of marriage, family, gender, and sexuality. From the Catholic perspective, homosexual practice is one more example of such a thing.

The analogy used above implies not only that social stigma is proper if something is immoral, but also that homosexuality (presented as an alternate and normal lifestyle) might just be another phenomenon which is merely trendy and fashionable, and that Christian traditionalists are right about its wrongness and abnormality. The political left, after all, is advocating almost all of these practices, or else a lessening or abolition of the social stigmas against them.

Radical, anti-traditional social love to co-opt people for their ends. They especially love to enlist religious people for their cause. That is one of the oldest tricks in the book, strategy-wise. They produce trendy clergy as spokesmen (the more denominations the better), so that they can say that the other religious people who oppose their viewpoint comprise the lunatic "fundamentalist" or "extremist" or "religious fanatic" fringe and don't speak for all Christians, etc.

This tactic has been used in almost every social change in the last few generations. It doesn't help that many entire Christian denominations have jumped on the bandwagon and actually adopted moral codes and ethical standards that they themselves formerly opposed. In a word, they have caved in to modernity and secularist ideologies.

No Christian can justify any violence or hatred against homosexual persons, but if a lifestyle is considered immoral by the great majority of the public, we would expect to see some manifestation of social disapproval. This will include, unfortunately and tragically, the haters and fringe figures who don't represent Christianity in any way, shape, or form (though some of these try to pretend that they do). Christians could pick the very worst example of homosexual activists (say, that crazy group that blasphemed at a Mass in St. Patrick's Cathedral in New York City a few years back), if we wanted to engage in this sort of rhetorical tactic. But that would be as wrong as all the stereotypes of "homophobia," and so forth.

Discrimination itself is already illegal, across the board, and should be. Many Christians are angry, however, about more-or-less forced acceptance of homosexual acts and lifestyle, when it goes against their religious beliefs. This is quite unfair. People can't be forced to believe things against their wills. Am I supposed to, for example, blithely accept the behavior of a drunk person (after all, there is evidence that a genetic predisposition exists for that condition also)? Am I supposed to consider his drunk driving or rude comments as perfectly normal and praiseworthy, as an alternate lifestyle?

Even if a homosexual orientation were innate, genetic, or not initiated by the person at all, that doesn't prove it is therefore "normal." Down's Syndrome is not considered normal, even though the person involved didn't cause it (and it is genetically-caused). Thalidomide babies born without arms were not "normal." Siamese Twins are not "normal." Hemophilia is not normal.

People have an inherent sense of what *normal* means. If something is widely regarded as unnatural, it is neither unreasonable nor wrong for a society to frown upon public (and especially, legally-sanctioned) expressions of such an abnormal lifestyle. In the name of tolerance and revulsion at others' "intolerance," some homosexual and other radical social activists are as intolerant as they can be of the Christian's right to hold whatever moral views we feel are taught to us by our religion.

Supposedly the political left and radical activists believe that "you can't legislate morality" (since they remind the rest of us of that, all the time). No one can be forced to love. But traditional Christians and Catholics should refuse to accept the false dichotomy that we allegedly don't love someone because we don't agree with some sin in their life. We don't love people by acquiescing in their sins. We must act upon what we believe, too.

Society is also quite hostile these days to Catholics, evangelical Protestants (especially white males from the south), political conservatives, non-feminists, creationists, and pro-lifers. I suspect that it is not all that different for the homosexual: the opposition is simply more widespread, as more people disagree morally with their lifestyle – and intensely at that. I agree that homosexuals have a terrible road to walk down. I would disagree as to the causes and nature of those difficulties, and the supposed total "innocence" of the homosexual.

Modern secular and increasingly barbarian America (and Europe is far worse) regularly caricatures and slanders people in the above-mentioned categories. Anti-Catholicism is still quite prevalent, even respectable in some circles, and produces a host of conspiratorial scenarios and other such silly nonsense. Conservatives are regularly slandered as uncompassionate, greedy, bigots, anti-Semites; non-feminists are chauvinist pigs and Neanderthals, creationists are dumb and stupid - on a par with flat-earthers --, and pro-lifers are anti-woman, callous to the needs of poor women and children, and go around murdering abortionists.

Homosexuals, then, are not the only ones who have to endure unjust treatment, in society (and I didn't even mention those in minority racial and ethnic groups who are still subject to a great deal of prejudice). That said, I do agree, however, that prejudice against homosexuals is a particularly virulent, ugly, and malicious strain of bigotry. I disagree about the commonly asserted *causation* of this: that it is *intrinsically* related to Christianity (simply because Christianity holds practicing homosexuality to be immoral).

Catholics are taught to love homosexual persons, but not to condone their sin. Christian conscience and Tradition will not allow that. The Catholic Church is not in the business of adopting viewpoints simply to be popular, fashionable, and "politically correct." *Real* tolerance is loving people *despite* profound disagreements -- not pretending that all is relative, and that all judgments whatever are improper in the first place.

If there is no God and hence no natural law, and no "ontological reality and meaning" of properly ordered sexuality, no sexual practice would be wrong, or sinful, or immoral. Men would simply be animals, and who cares what orifice is used for whatever purpose?

Blaise Pascal stated in his famous *Pensees*, that when men reject God they do one of two things: they exalt themselves up to the level of gods, or they debase themselves to the level of animals. On the other hand, if there is a God and a revelation, homosexuals need to honestly face those facts, and submit themselves to the moral teaching of that God, just like the rest of us do. It is no bed of roses to live a chaste heterosexual life, either -- whether married or single -- these days.

Catholics have a moral objection to homosexual sexual practices, which are almost always present -- I assume -- in a so-called "gay marriage." No one cares if men live together or "love" each other (Jonathan and David did that) as long as they don't commit sodomy or other sinful sexual practices. This is the Catholic position. Sodomy should be outlawed on health grounds alone, if not also on moral, religious, and philosophical grounds.

A homosexual with whom I was dialoguing stated, "Nothing which exists in nature is unnatural." I replied by contending that by this logic, he could have intercourse with a hog, or a baboon, or a duck-billed platypus (if indeed that is possible). or stick his toe up someone's nose, or his elbow in their ear. Poisonous mushrooms are natural. Does that mean someone should eat them? Swamps are natural. Should we drink from them, or take a bath in one? Niagara Falls is entirely natural, but if I take a boat ride over it, certain consequences will have to be faced.

Chapter Six

Radical Feminism

One reason for the male-only priesthood (an issue which is often raised by radical feminists) is very straightforward and should be uncontroversial. Jesus Christ was a Man. Given the fact that every validly ordained priest functions as an *alter Christus* at Mass (since, according to Catholic theology, it is Christ Himself who transforms the elements and performs the supernatural consecration, not the priest, who "stands in" for Him), it is altogether appropriate that men only are ordained.

Of course we also have clear instructions and examples of Scripture which ought to be sufficient in and of themselves to settle this question. None of the twelve disciples were women. Jesus must have had a good reason for that, whether or not we understand it. The Christian trusts Jesus and apostolic, Christian Tradition, rather than the fads and fancies of our post-modern, sexually libertine age.

The highest of God's created beings, and the only sinless creature who ever lived -- according to Catholicism -- is a woman (the Blessed Virgin Mary), and a woman first saw the risen Jesus (Mary Magdalene: John 20:11-18). No man -- by virtue of "unfair" biology -- ever had the immense, unfathomable honor of "bearing God" (*Theotokos*) and thus entering into incomprehensible biological intimacy with Deity. Protestants object to the alleged Catholic veneration of Mary as next to God, while feminists excoriate the Catholic Church for lowering the status of women vis a vis men. Ironies never cease.

God gave the Blessed Virgin Mary the special grace of sinlessness and removal of original sin (the Immaculate Conception). Now if He could do that for her, why not for *men* too? We've been treated unfairly! At least God could have caused Joseph or Paul or David or Moses to be without sin. This is *so* unfair! Why did men have to be created so unequal and inferior to women? If women get to have a created Mediatrix and Queen of Heaven as a "role model," why can't men have one of *our* kind in such a lofty estate? Jesus doesn't count because He is the Creator, not a creature like us.

The last paragraph is an example of the classical logical technique of *argumentum ad absurdum*, which attempts to show that the logical consequences of a position lead to absurdity and nonsense; in this instance, certain radical feminist complaints applied to Catholic theology and men.

There is no notion of inequality involved in a male-only priesthood, since if that were the case, it is neither likely nor plausible that God would raise Mary to her supremely exalted state (as she is a creature). If anything -- in light of that fact -- it might be stated (only slightly tongue-in-cheek) that Christianity teaches the superiority of *women*, not men.

Even beyond the Blessed Virgin, there are plenty of women role models in Catholic history to look up to and emulate: St. Teresa of Avila, or St. Catherine of Siena (who rebuked popes), or St. Therese of Liseux, or St. Clare, or St. Hildegard of Bingen, or Mother Teresa, or Dorothy Day, or St. Edith Stein, or Deborah, Esther, Ruth, and many other biblical heroines.

Catholicism, and Christianity in general, does not teach any gender inequality whatsoever (see, for example, Galatians 3:28: *There is neither Jew nor Greek, . . . slave nor free, . . . male nor female; for you are all one in Christ Jesus*). If women are unequal to men in orthodox (i.e., Nicene and Chalcedonian) Christianity of whatever stripe, then Jesus is not equal to the Father, since He subjected Himself to the Father (Philippians 2:5-8) and even to Mary and Joseph (Luke 2:51).

The Holy Trinity is a very apt analogy because it offers a clear example of an equality that nevertheless includes (by its very nature) subjection and differential roles -- exactly analogous to marriage and male ordination. Thus, radical feminism logically leads to heterodoxy with regard to the Holy Trinity, or else undue skepticism towards the Bible. That is perhaps one reason why why sexual and theological liberalism are so closely allied.

God could have made both fathers and mothers produce milk, so I could have had the "equality" and closeness and "parental bond" of nursing my four children when they were babies, like my wife did. But He chose not to and I accept His wisdom in that.

He also could have not only called all to the priesthood regardless of gender, but saved all, if He had so chosen, without having to take on flesh and thus subject Himself (in His Human Nature) to the limitations of human beings. Jesus chose to be "unequal" to the Father (Philippians 2:6-11). Perhaps we should protest that inequality ought to be stamped out even in the highest levels of heaven? Away with the suffering Messiah and the "oppressed" Jesus, who is being exploited by the Father?

"Maleness" and "femaleness" mean much more than mere possession of certain genitalia. Rather, they are complete roles and ontological realities created by God. Orthodox, traditional Christians aren't the ones who are hung up on maleness; rather it is the "gender radicals" who favor women's ordination. We are quite content to accept the fact that God came to earth as a Man and taught His disciples and recorded in His inspired Revelation that only men ought to be ordained, just as He gave Mary the unfathomable honor and privilege of bearing God and serving in a sublime way as a Mediatrix and Spiritual Mother.

Many feminists would assert that men and women are different physiologically, yet not in any other way They are supposedly exactly the same, except for the sexual element, where they are simply "yin and yang," "positive and negative," etc. But God has informed us differently as to "ontological difference": 1 Peter 3:7, 1 Corinthians 11:3,7-9, 1 Timothy 2:12-14, Ephesians 5:22-25.

Perhaps "unisexists" object also to the fact that God the Father chose to become incarnate in a male body? Maybe God should have come as a sexless eunuch or a woman? And on what basis can mere fallen human beings (of either gender) question the will and wisdom of Almighty God? I'm sure many of this mindset justify their views by the questioning of Holy Scripture (either its content, or its faithful manuscript transmission). But in this instance, I'm not aware of any scholar, however unorthodox, who denies that Jesus was a man.

The Church of Christ can't call someone who isn't given a certain gift and vocation -- by virtue of God's will and "spiritual ontology," so to speak, any more than it could call me to bear a child and suckle it after birth. This "unisexist" mentality is in outright denial that there is an ordained, God-created and -willed, ontological difference between men and women. As such, it directly challenges divine prerogatives, and as such, must be fought against and refuted at all costs.

In the course of one of my online dialogues, my discussion opponent asserted that Jesus didn't choose women disciples because he knew women wouldn't be accepted in that period by the Jews. But this is, of course, sheer speculation and nothing more, with no biblical support; nor is it very plausible at all. Since when did Jesus care a whit about what anyone would think of His actions and teaching, anyway? No one can observe His constant battles with (and rebukes of) the Pharisees and conclude that He had any thought of conforming His ideas (Truth) to their pet beliefs and "golden cows."

Furthermore, why would Jesus forgive an adulteress publicly (John 8:1-11), speak to the Samaritan woman at the well (John 4:4-29), accept financial support from several women (Mark 15:40-41), let women anoint His feet with their hair (John 12:1-8; Matthew 26:6-13) and first see Him resurrected, etc., if He was at all worried about the "acceptance" of women or "chauvinism" among the Jews of that time and culture?

Jesus wasn't bound by pragmatic and "peer pressure" considerations, as so many of us are. He clearly treated women as equals to men, so that if He intended for them to be ordained like men, it is altogether plausible to assume He certainly would have made that teaching publicly also. The Pharisees objected to all these things just as much as many vainly imagine that the Catholic Church wants to "keep women out" of the priesthood out of bigotry and chauvinism rather than obedience to God's decrees.

My correspondent then made the charge that "Rome" was slow to recognize feminine equality, while many other Christians denominations are "enlightened" and therefore ordain women. But how long have these other "branches" ordained women? And why did they wait so long? Did they need the "illumination" of radical feminism and the sexual revolution to "wake up" and "see the light?" Are we now in a sufficiently enlightened age to finally grasp what sexual liberals and feminists apparently think is self-evident, while ages past were hopelessly regressive and "primitive?" It is the height of arrogance and folly for any of us moderns, with multiple hundreds of millions of dead in our century and enough slaughtered preborn children to fill up Yankee Stadium to the brim, field and all, to wax eloquent about our "progressive" understanding of men and women!

It is utterly implausible to think that a century as corrupt and evil as the 20th (hence, Communism, Naziism, and abortion as the quintessential examples of this, just as slavery and genocide of the Indians were in the 19th century) would be the one to discover these moral truths which sexual liberals consider so self-evident. It just doesn't make any sense. Of all the twenty centuries since Christ, we are the ones to discover the "truth" that men and women are essentially no different from each other (or that abortion is morally permissible), and that virtually all Christians previously were dolts and misogynists, who couldn't see that women ought to be ordained?!

The "subjection" of wives to husbands has also been a controversial point for all sorts of feminists, and indeed, for many women, generally speaking, who are in an abusive situation, or who don't properly understand the entire biblical and Pauline context of this teaching. That wives should be *subject to their husbands* (Ephesians 5:22), is (biblically) undeniable. Biblical or Church teaching cannot change in any *essential* way. But one must interpret and apply that command, as Pope John Paul II does in the following excerpt from his *Apostolic Letter On the Dignity and Vocation of Women* (1988):

> *Wives, be subject to your husbands, as to the Lord. For the husband is the head of the wife* (Eph 5:22-23). The author knows that this way of speaking, so profoundly rooted in the customs and religious traditions of the time, is to be understood and carried out in a new way: as a *mutual subjection out of reverence for Christ* (cf. Eph 5:21). This is especially true because the husband is called the *head* of the wife as Christ is the head of the Church; he is so in order to give *himself up for her* (Eph 5:25), and giving himself up for her means giving up even his own life. However, whereas in the relationship between Christ and the Church the subjection is only on the part of the Church, in the relationship between husband and wife the *subjection* is not one-sided but mutual. (section 24)

This is an honest grappling with Paul's teaching in its Ephesian context and in its entirety, such as Galatians 3:28 (. . . *there is no longer male and female*). Indeed, an element of matrimonial subjection exists, in which the husband has the final say in decision-making, in relatively rare instances where there is an unresolved disagreement.

Yet the pope incorporates the injunction of mutual subjection in Ephesians 5:21 into his teaching, which is also the tradition of the Church, for far too often husbands have abused their God-given prerogatives, which are rooted in creation itself, ontology and the inherent nature of things. Men (males/husbands) have *not* often acted like Jesus Christ did, in His total self-sacrifice and unconditional love. They have *not* very often truly loved and served their wives like Christ loved the Church. *The greatest among you will be your servant* (Matthew 23:11).

The two shall become one flesh.

(Matthew 19:5 / Ephesians 5:31)

In the same way husbands should love their wives as they do their own bodies. He who loves his wife loves himself. For no one ever hates his own body, but he nourishes and tenderly cares for it, just as Christ does for the church, because we are members of his body.

(Ephesians 5:28-30)

The teaching of subjection has -- most tragically -- been distorted; abused by men for their own selfish purposes of pride, power, and the subjugation of women. This is wicked, and it is not biblical. The pope and the Catholic Church have preserved the traditional Christian and biblical teaching, as well as other traditional morals such as the prohibition of divorce, contraception, abortion, a female priesthood, and homosexuality.

Some Protestant strains of thought have mistakenly interpreted the Ephesians passage and other related ones in the sense of an absolute, abject subjection of the wife to the husbands' wishes (and too often, unreasonable demands). But, as shown, this is unbiblical and contrary to St. Paul's clear teaching in Ephesians 5:21,28, and Galatians 3:28. As a result, radical egalitarian feminism (not the legitimate variety which espouses equal pay, etc.) has sprung up in reaction largely because of the sins and wickedness of men, and the sanction of the same by various Christian denominations. One sin leads to a greater sin.

Pope John Paul II was equally wise and eloquent in his Angelus of 8 March, 1998:

> 1. Today "Woman's Day" is being celebrated in many countries of the world. It is an important event which invites us to reflect on women's role in society, and even prior to that, in God's plan. Recognition of this role has encountered numerous obstacles in history. Even today it cannot be said that all resistance has been overcome.
>
> I gladly take this opportunity to express the hope that woman's equal dignity will at last be fully recognized and her particular gifts adequately appreciated. Man and woman complement each other not only physically and psychologically at the level of behavior, but more profoundly at the level of being. Everyone knows

Catholic doctrine on this subject, which I have often had occasion to recall, especially in my Apostolic Letter *Mulieris Dignitatem* and the *Letter to Women*.

2. We are unfortunately heirs to a history of enormous conditioning that has hindered the progress of women: their dignity is sometimes ignored, their special qualities misrepresented and they themselves are frequently marginalized. This has prevented them from being truly themselves and has deprived the whole human race of authentic spiritual riches.

How many women have been and are still valued more for their physical appearance than for their personal qualities, professional competence, intellectual work, the richness of their sensitivity and, finally, for the very dignity of their being!

And what can be said then of the obstacles that in so many parts of the world still prevent women from being fully involved in social, political and economic life? In this regard, while recalling that the 50th anniversary of the *Universal Declaration of Human Rights* is being celebrated this year, I wish to make an appeal on behalf of women whose basic rights are still denied today by the political regimes of their countries: women who are segregated, forbidden to study or to exercise a profession, or even to express their thoughts in public. May international solidarity hasten the due recognition of their rights.

3. May Mary, the model of a fulfilled woman, help everyone, especially all women, to understand the "feminine genius", not only to carry out God's precise plan, but also to make more room for women in the various areas of social life.

May Mary present to the Lord the expectations and prayers, the commitment and sufferings of all the women of the world, and may she show her motherly concern to every man and woman on the path of life.

Moving on from Catholic and Christian theology of gender, to a more sociological and anthropological analysis, it is quite arguable that women have been the greatest victims of the sexual revolution that radical feminism helped in part to produce and extol. Most women have succumbed to the self-serving male notion that they must engage in sex before marriage. In so doing they have yielded up their most precious asset: themselves and their most intimate "secrets."

Men now expect virtually all women to engage in sexual activity relatively early in relationships (and women have tragically bought into that, thus making themselves "objects" -- even more so). In the Christian view, it was assumed that women would "hold out" this "reward" for the man who would renounce his passions in exchange for love and the long-term benefits accruing from a committed, lifetime relationship. Men are certainly habitually (and characteristically) guilty of having ulterior motives when it comes to getting to know women (sexually).

The sexual revolution has only greatly exacerbated that immemorial problem for women. They have bought, hook, line, and sinker, the traditional, older-than-the-hills exploitative sexual tactics of men. Once women were hoodwinked by that, many of our current societal woes became inevitable. Certainly people aren't happier because of this so-called sexual "liberation." That much is certain.

We've seen the fruit of the sexual revolution: broken hearts and homes, abortion-on-demand, shattered lives, illegitimacy, STDs, more rape (including "date rape"), more child abuse, more sexual perversion, pornography, child molestation, wife-beating, crime and drugs resulting therefrom, sexual harassment, etc., *ad infinitum*. And yet the social libertarians and radical feminists assert that this is a better, happier, "sexual world" than the one which was cultivated by the Christian

Church for multiple hundreds of years? The greatest irony is that studies have consistently shown that practicing Christians have a far more fulfilling and rewarding sex life than their "wild" counterparts who fell for the lie of "try before you buy."

There seems to be a growing realization on all sides that the world of "liberalism," libertinism, moral relativism, and so-called "liberation" and "(sexual) freedom" has not turned out to be the Utopia which was foolishly hoped for. Traditional Christians knew this full well all along, of course, but cultures invariably have to learn the hard way -- that's one of the things history teaches us.

People never change. Sexual chastity was just as difficult in times past as it is now. The difference is that now we have the sanction of liberal religion, agreeing with secularism that several or all of these things are now okay (hence, calling evil good), because we are now "progressive" and "enlightened."

The current chaos and wholesale destruction of the family and moral values, is largely due to faulty views of sexuality and marriage. Who will argue with a straight face that the post-Christian society we now have is in any sense morally, institutionally, emotionally, or spiritually superior to what preceded it? If someone has, I would love to see it.

Have men habitually dominated and brutalized women? Of course; no one would deny that. But the traditional Christian view of women is the best thing that ever happened to them. This is most clear when the Christian view is contrasted to pagan and non-Christian religious viewpoints, with regard to women. In ancient Rome (and I believe, Greece), the husband basically "owned" the wife, as if a slave. We see more or less utter subordination of women in Muslim countries, self-immolation of widows in Hindu cultures, aborting of female babies in China (sex selection abortion) and also forced abortion, and the routine cruel clitorectomies of Africa. Even in ancient Israel (according to the rabbinic school of Hillel), a wife could be sent packing at a moment's notice, for something as trivial as making bad dinners. It took Christianity to radically change all these hideous, grossly unjust practices.

Appendix One

G.K. Chesterton on Sex and Contraception:

The Surrender Upon Sex / Babies and Distributism / Sex and Property / Social Reform Versus Birth Control

[First three selections from: *The Well and the Shallows*, New York: Sheed & Ward, 1935, pp. 37-44, 142-146, 232-236; the last selection was originally two articles for *Lansbury's Labour Weekly*; published together as a pamphlet in the same year: 1927]

THE SURRENDER UPON SEX

I have explained that these are sketches of six separate occasions, on which I should have become a Catholic, if I had not been the one and only kind of human being who cannot become a Catholic. The excitement of conversion is still open to the atheist and the diabolist; and everybody can be converted except the convert. In my first outline, I mentioned that one of the crises, which would in any case have driven me the way I had gone already, was the shilly-shallying and sham liberality of the famous Lambeth Report on what is quaintly called Birth Control. It is in fact, of course, a scheme for preventing birth in order to escape control. But this particular case was only the culmination of a long process of compromise and cowardice about the problem of sex; the final surrender after a continuous retreat.

There is one historical human fact which now seems to me so plain and solid, that I think that even if I were to lose the Faith, I could not lose sight of the fact. It has rather the character of a fact of chemistry or geology; though from another side it is mysterious enough, like many other manifest and unmistakable facts. It is this: that at the moment when Religion lost touch with Rome, it changed instantly and internally, from top to bottom, in its very substance and the stuff of which it was made. It changed in substance; it did not necessarily change in form or features or externals. It might do the same things; but it could not be the same thing. It might go on saying the same things; but it was not the same thing that was saying them. At the very beginning, indeed, the situation was almost exactly like that. Henry VIII was a Catholic in everything except that he was not a Catholic. He observed everything down to the last bead and candle; he accepted everything down to the last deduction from a definition; he accepted everything except Rome. And in that instant of refusal, his religion became a different religion; a different sort of religion; a different sort of thing. In that instant it began to change; and it has not stopped changing yet. We are all somewhat wearily aware that some Modern Churchmen call such continuous change progress; as when we remark that a corpse crawling with worms has an increased vitality; or that a snow-man, slowly turning into a puddle, is purifying itself of its accretions. But I am not concerned with this argument here. The point is that a dead man may look like a sleeping man a moment after he is dead; but decomposition has actually begun. The point is that the snow-man may in theory be made in the real image of man. Michelangelo made a statue in snow; and it might quite easily have been an exact replica of one of his statues in marble; but it was not in marble. Most probably the snow-man has begun to melt almost as soon as it is made. But even if the frost holds, it is still a stuff capable of melting when the frost goes. It seemed to many that Protestantism would long continue to be, in the popular phrase, a perfect frost. But that does not alter the difference between ice and marble; and marble does not melt.

The same sort of progressives are always telling us to have a trust in the Future. As a fact, the one thing that a progressive cannot possibly have is a trust in the Future. He cannot have a trust in his own Future; let alone in his own Futurism. If he sets no limit to change, it may change all his own progressive views as much as his conservative views. It was so with the Church first founded by Henry VIII; who was, in almost everything commonly cursed as Popery, rather more Popish than the Pope. He thought he might trust it to go on being orthodox; to go on being sacramentalist; to go on being sacerdotalist; to go on being ritualist, and the rest. There was only one little weakness. It could not trust itself to go on being itself. Nothing else, except the Faith, can trust itself to go on being itself.

Now touching this truth in relation to Sex, I may be permitted to introduce a trivial journalistic anecdote. A few years before the War, some of my fellow-journalists, Socialists as well as Tories, were questioning me about what I really meant by Democracy; and especially if I really thought there was anything in Rousseau's idea of the General Will. I said I thought (and I think I still think) that there can be such a thing, but it must be much more solid and unanimous than a mere majority, such as rules in party politics. I applied the old phrase of the Man in the Street, by saying that if I looked out of the window at a strange man walking past my house, I could bet heavily on his thinking some things, but not the common controversial things The Liberals might have a huge majority, but he need not be a Liberal; statistics might prove England to be preponderantly Conservative, but I would not bet a button that he would be Conservative. But (I said) I should bet that he believes in wearing clothes. And my Socialist questioners did not question this; they, too, accepted clothes as so universal an agreement of common sense and civilisation, that we might attribute the tradition to a total stranger, unless he were a lunatic. Such a little while ago! To-day, when I see the stranger walking down the street, I should not bet that he believes even in clothes. The country is dotted with Nudist Colonies; the bookstalls are littered with Nudist magazines; the papers swarm with polite little paragraphs, praising the brownness and braveness of the special sort of anarchical asses here in question. At any given moment, there may be a General Will; but it is an uncommonly weak and wavering sort of will, without the Faith to support it.

As in that one matter of modesty, or the mere externals of sex, so in all the deeper matters of sex, the modern will has been amazingly weak and wavering. And I suppose it is because the Church has known from the first this weakness which we have all discovered at last, that about certain sexual matters She has been very decisive and dogmatic; as many good people have quite honestly thought, too decisive and dogmatic. Now a Catholic is a person who has plucked up courage to face the incredible and inconceivable idea that something else may be wiser than he is. And the most striking and outstanding illustration is perhaps to be found in the Catholic view of marriage as compared with the modern theory of divorce; not, it must be noted, the very modern theory of divorce, which is the mere negation of marriage; but even more the slightly less modern and more moderate theory of divorce, which was generally accepted even when I was a boy. This is the very vital point or test of the question; for it explains the Church's rejection of the moderate as well as the immoderate theory. It illustrates the very fact I am pointing out, that Divorce has already turned into something totally different from what was intended, even by those who first proposed it. Already we must think ourselves back into a different world of thought, in order to understand how anybody ever thought it was compatible with Victorian virtue; and many very virtuous Victorians did. But they only tolerated this social solution as an exception; and many other modern social solutions they would not have tolerated at all. My own parents were not even orthodox Puritans or High Church people; they were Universalists more akin to Unitarians. But they would have regarded Birth-Prevention exactly as they would have regarded Infanticide. Yet about Divorce such liberal Protestants did hold an intermediate view, which was substantially this. They thought the normal necessity and duty of all married people was to remain faithful to their marriage; that this could be demanded of them, like common honesty or any other virtue. But they thought that in some very extreme and extraordinary cases a divorce was allowable. Now, putting aside our own mystical and sacramental doctrine, this was not, on the face of it, an unreasonable position. It certainly was not meant to be an anarchical position. But the Catholic Church, standing almost alone, declared that it would in fact lead to an anarchical position; and the Catholic Church was right.

Any man with eyes in his head, whatever the ideas in his head, who looks at the world as it is to-day, must know that the whole social substance of marriage has changed; just as the whole social substance of Christianity changed with the divorce of Henry VIII. As in the other case, the externals remained for a time and some of them remain still. Some divorced persons, who can be married quite legally by a registrar, go on complaining bitterly that they cannot be married by a priest. They regard a church as a peculiarly suitable place in which to make and break the same vow at the same moment. And the Bishop of London, who was supposed to sympathise with the more sacramental party, recently submitted to such a demand on the ground that it was a very special case. As if every human being's case were not a special case. That decision was one of the occasions on which I should have done a bolt, if I had delayed it so long. But the general social atmosphere is much the most important matter. Numbers of normal people are getting married, thinking already that they may be divorced. The instant that idea enters, the whole conception of the old Protestant compromise vanishes. The sincere and innocent Victorian would never have married a woman reflecting that he could divorce her. He would as soon have married a woman reflecting that he could murder her. These things were not supposed to be among the daydreams of the honeymoon. The psychological substance of the whole thing has altered; the marble has turned to ice; and the ice has melted with most amazing rapidity. The Church was right to refuse even the exception. The world has admitted the exception; and the exception has become the rule.

As I have said, the weak and inconclusive pronouncement upon Birth-Prevention was only the culmination of this long intellectual corruption. I need not discuss the particular problem again at this point; beyond saying that the same truth applies as in the case of Divorce. People propose an easy way out of certain human responsibilities and difficulties; including a way out of the responsibility and difficulty of doing economic justice and achieving better payment for the poor. But these people propose this easy method, in the hope that some people will only use it to a moderate extent; whereas it is much more probable that an indefinite number will use it to an indefinite extent. It is odd that they do not see this; because the writers and thinkers among them are no longer by any means optimistic about human nature, like Rousseau; but much more pessimistic about human nature than we are. Considering mankind as described, for instance, by Mr. Aldous Huxley, it is hard to see what answer he could possibly give, except the answer which we give, if the question were put thus: "On the one side, there is an easy way out of the difficulty by avoiding childbirth: on the other side, there is a very difficult way out of the difficulty, by reconstructing the whole social system and toiling and perhaps fighting for the better system. Which way are the men you describe more likely to take?" But my concern is not with open and direct opponents like Mr. Huxley; but with all to whom I might once have looked to defend the country of the Christian altars. They ought surely to know that the foe now on the frontiers offers no terms of compromise; but threatens a complete destruction. And they have sold the pass.

BABIES AND DISTRIBUTISM

I hope it is not a secret arrogance to say that I do not think I am exceptionally arrogant; or if I were, my religion would prevent me from being proud of my pride. Nevertheless, for those of such a philosophy, there is a very terrible temptation to intellectual pride, in the welter of wordy and worthless philosophies that surround us to-day. Yet there are not many things that move me to anything like a personal contempt. I do not feel any contempt for an atheist, who is often a man limited and constrained by his own logic to a very sad simplification. I do not feel any contempt for a Bolshevist, who is a man driven to the same-negative simplification by a revolt against very positive wrongs. But there is one type of person for whom I feel what I can only call contempt. And that is the popular propagandist of what he or she absurdly describes as Birth-Control.

I despise Birth-Control first because it is a weak and wobbly and cowardly word. It is also an entirely meaningless word; and is used so as to curry favour even with those who would at first recoil from its real meaning. The proceeding these quack doctors recommend does not *control* any birth. It only makes sure that there shall never be any birth to control. It cannot, for instance, determine sex, or even make any selection in the style of the pseudo-science of Eugenics. Normal people can only act so as to produce birth; and these people can only act so as to prevent birth. But these people know perfectly well that they dare not write the plain word Birth-Prevention, in any one of the hundred places where they write the hypocritical word Birth-Control. They know as well as I do that the very word Birth-Prevention would strike a chill into the public, the instant it was blazoned on headlines, or proclaimed on platforms, or scattered in advertisements like any other quack medicine. They dare not call it by its name, because its name is very bad advertising. Therefore they use a conventional and unmeaning word, which may make the quack medicine sound more innocuous.

Second, I despise Birth-Control because it is a weak and wobbly and cowardly thing. It is not even a step along the muddy road they call Eugenics; it is a flat refusal to take the first and most obvious step along the road of Eugenics. Once grant that their philosophy is right, and their course of action is obvious; and they dare not take it; they dare not even declare it. If there is no authority in things which Christendom has called moral, because their origins were mystical, then they are clearly free to ignore all difference between animals and men; and treat men as we treat animals. They need not palter with the stale and timid compromise and convention called Birth-Control. Nobody applies it to the cat. The obvious course for Eugenists is to act towards babies as they act towards kittens. Let all the babies be born and then let us drown those we do not like. I cannot see any objection to it; except the moral or mystical sort of objection that we advance against Birth-Prevention. And that would be real and even reasonable Eugenics; for we could then select the best, or at least the healthiest, and sacrifice what are called the unfit. By the weak compromise of Birth-Prevention, we are very probably sacrificing the fit and only producing the unfit. The births we prevent may be the births of the best and most beautiful children; those we allow, the weakest or worst. Indeed, it is probable; for the habit discourages the early parentage of young and vigorous people; and lets them put off the experience to later years, mostly from mercenary motives. Until I see a real pioneer and progressive leader coming out with a good, bold, scientific programme for drowning babies, I will not join the movement.

But there is a third, reason for my contempt, much deeper and therefore much more difficult to express; in which is rooted all my reasons for being anything I am or attempt to be; and above all, for being a Distributist. Perhaps the nearest to a description of it is to say this: that my contempt boils over into bad behaviour when I hear the common suggestion that a birth is avoided because people want to be "free" to go to the cinema or buy a gramophone or a loud-speaker. What makes me want to walk over such people like doormats is that they use the word "free." By every act of that sort they chain themselves to the most servile and mechanical system yet tolerated by men. The cinema is a machine for unrolling certain regular patterns called pictures; expressing the most vulgar millionaires' notion of the taste of the most vulgar millions. The gramophone is a machine for recording such tunes as certain shops and other organisations choose to sell. The wireless is better; but even that is marked by the modern mark of all three; the impotence of the receptive party. The amateur cannot challenge the actor; the householder will find it vain to go and shout into the gramophone; the mob cannot pelt the modern speaker, especially when he is a loud-speaker. It is all a central mechanism giving out to men exactly what their masters think they should have.

Now a child is the very sign and sacrament of personal freedom. He is a fresh free will added to the wills of the world; he is something that his parents have freely chosen to produce and which they freely agree to protect. They can feel that any amusement he gives (which is often considerable) really comes from him and from them, and from nobody else. He has been born without the intervention of any master or lord. He is a creation and a contribution; he is their own creative contribution to creation. He is also a much more beautiful, wonderful, amusing and astonishing thing than any of the stale stories or jingling jazz tunes turned out bv the machines. When men no longer feel that he is so, they have lost the appreciation of primary things, and therefore all sense of proportion about the world. People who prefer the mechanical pleasures, to such a miracle, are jaded and enslaved. They are preferring the very dregs of life to the first fountains of life. They are preferring the last, crooked, indirect, borrowed, repeated and exhausted things of our dying Capitalist civilisation, to the reality which is the only rejuvenation of all civilisation. It is they who are hugging the chains of their old slavery; it is the child who is ready for the new world.

SEX AND PROPERTY

In the dull, dusty, stale, stiff-jointed and lumbering language, to which most modern discussion is limited, it is necessary to say that there is at this moment the same fashionable fallacy about Sex and about Property. In the older and freer language, in which men could both speak and sing, it is truer to say that the same evil spirit has blasted the two great powers that make the poetry of life; the Love of Woman and the Love of the Land. It is important to observe, to start with, that these two things were closely connected so long as humanity was human, even when it was heathen. Nay, they were still closely connected, even when it was a decadent heathenism. But even the stink of decaying heathenism has not been so bad as the stink of decaying Christianity. The corruption of the best....

For instance, there were throughout antiquity, both in its first stage and its last, modes of idolatry and imagery of which Christian men can hardly speak. "Let them not be so much as named among you." Men wallowed in the mere sexuality of a mythology of sex; they organised prostitution like priesthood, for the service of their temples; they made pornography their only poetry; they paraded emblems that turned even architecture into a sort of cold and colossal exhibitionism. Many learned books have been written of all these phallic cults; and anybody can go to them for the details, for all I care. But what interests me is this:

In one way all this ancient sin was infinitely superior, immeasurably superior, to the modern sin. All those who write of it at least agree on one fact; that it was the cult of Fruitfulness. It was unfortunately too often interwoven, very closely, with the cult of the fruitfulness of the land. It was at least on the side of Nature. It was at least on the side of Life. It has been left to the last Christians, or rather to the first Christians fully committed to blaspheming and denying Christianity, to invent a new kind of worship of Sex, which is not even a worship of Life. It has been left to the very latest Modernists to proclaim an erotic religion which at once exalts lust and forbids fertility. The new Paganism literally merits the reproach of Swinburne, when mourning for the old Paganism: "and rears not the bountiful token and spreads not the fatherly feast." The new priests abolish the fatherhood and keep the feast-to themselves. They are worse than Swinburne's Pagans. The priests of Priapus and Cotytto go into the kingdom of heaven before them.

Now it is not unnatural that this unnatural separation, between sex and fruitfulness, which even the Pagans would have thought a perversion, has been accompanied with a similar separation and perversion about the nature of the love of the land. In both departments there is precisely the same fallacy; which it is quite possible to state precisely. The reason why our contemporary countrymen do not understand what we mean by Property is that they only think of it in the sense of Money; in the sense of salary; in the sense of something which is immediately consumed, enjoyed and expended; something which gives momentary pleasure and disappears. They do not understand that we mean by Property something that includes that pleasure incidentally; but begins and ends with something far more grand and worthy and creative. The man who makes an orchard where there has been a field, who owns the orchard and decides to whom it shall descend, does also enjoy the taste of apples; and let us hope, also, the taste of cider. But he is doing something very much grander, and ultimately more gratifying, than merely eating an apple. He is imposing his will upon the world in the manner of the charter given him by the will of God; he is asserting that his soul is his own, and does not belong to the Orchard Survey Department, or the chief Trust in the Apple Trade. But he is also doing something which was implicit in all the most ancient religions of the earth; in those great panoramas of pageantry and ritual that followed the order of the seasons in China or Babylonia; he is worshipping the fruitfulness of the world. Now the notion of narrowing property merely to *enjoying* money is exactly like the notion of narrowing love merely to *enjoying* sex. In both cases an incidental, isolated, servile and even secretive pleasure is substituted for participation in a great creative process; even in the everlasting Creation of the world.

The two sinister things can be seen side by side in the system of Bolshevist Russia; for Communism is the only complete and logical working model of Capitalism. The sins are there a system which are everywhere else a sort of repeated blunder. From the first, it is admitted, that the whole system was directed towards encouraging or driving the worker to spend his wages; to have nothing left on the next pay day; to enjoy everything and consume everything and efface everything; in short, to shudder at the thought of only one crime; the creative crime of thrift. It was a tame extravagance; a sort of disciplined dissipation; a meek and submissive prodigality. For the moment the slave left off drinking all his wages, the moment he began to hoard or hide any property, he would be saving up something which might ultimately purchase his liberty. He might begin to count for something in the State; that is, he might become less of a slave and more of a citizen. Morally considered, there has been nothing quite so unspeakably mean as this Bolshevist generosity. But it will be noted that exactly the same spirit and tone pervades the manner of dealing with the other matter. Sex also is to come to the slave merely as a pleasure; that it may never be a power. He is to know as little as possible, or at least to think as little as possible, of the pleasure as anything else except a pleasure; to think or know nothing of where it comes from or where it will go to, when once the soiled object has passed through his own hands. He is not to trouble about its origin in the purposes of God or its sequel in the posterity of man. In every department he is not a possessor, but only a consumer; even if it be of the first elements of life and fire in so far as they are consumable; he is to have no notion of the sort of Burning Bush that burns and is not consumed. For that bush only grows on the soil, on the real land where human beings can behold it; and the spot on which they stand is holy ground. Thus there is an exact parallel between the two modern moral, or immoral, ideas of social reform. The world has forgotten simultaneously that the making of a Farm is something much larger than the making of a profit, or even a product, in the sense of liking the taste of beetroot sugar; and that the founding of a Family is something much larger than sex in the limited sense of. current literature; which was anticipated in one bleak and blinding flash in a single line of George Meredith; "And eat our pot of honey on the grave."

SOCIAL REFORM VERSUS BIRTH CONTROL

The real history of the world is full of the queerest cases of notions that have turned clean head-over-heels and completely contradicted themselves. The last example is an extraordinary notion that what is called Birth Control is a social reform that goes along with other social reforms favoured by progressive people.

It is rather like saying that cutting off King Charles' head was one of the most elegant of the Cavalier fashions in hair-dressing. It is like saying that decapitation is an advance on dentistry. It may or may not be right to cut off the King's head; it may or may not be right to cut off your own head when you have the toothache. But anybody ought to be able to see that if we once simplify things by head cutting we can do without hair-cutting; that it will be needless to practise dentistry on the dead or philanthropy on the unborn--or the unbegotten. So it is not a provision for our descendants to say that the destruction of our descendants will render it unnecessary to provide them with anything. It may be that it is only destruction in the sense of negation; and it may be that few of our descendants may be allowed to survive. But it is obvious that the negation is a piece of mere pessimism, opposing itself to the more optimistic notion that something can be done for the whole family of man. Nor is it surprising to anybody who can think, to discover that this is exactly what really happened.

The story began with Godwin, the friend of Shelley, and the founder of so many of the social hopes that are called revolutionary. Whatever we think of his theory in detail, he certainly filled the more generous youth of his time with that thirst for social justice and equality which is the inspiration of Socialism and other ideals. What is even more gratifying, he filled the wealthy old men of his time with pressing and enduring terror, and about three-quarters of the talk of Tories and Whigs of that time consists of sophistries and excuses invented to patch up a corrupt compromise of oligarchy against the appeal to fraternity and fundamental humanity made by men like Godwin and Shelley.

Malthus: An answer to Godwin

The old oligarchs would use any tool against the new democrats; and one day it was their dismal good luck to get hold of a tool called Malthus. Malthus wrote avowedly and admittedly an answer to Godwin. His whole dreary book was only intended to be an answer to Godwin. Whereas Godwin was trying to show that humanity might be made happier and more humane, Malthus was trying to show that humanity could never by any possibility be made happier or more humane. The argument he used was this: that if the starving man were made tolerably free or fairly prosperous, he would marry and have a number of children, and there would not be food for all. The inference was, evidently, that he must be left to starve. The point about the increase of children he fortified by a fantastically mathematical formula about geometrical progression, which any living human being can clearly see is inapplicable to any living thing. Nothing depending on the human will can proceed by geometrical progression, and population certainly does not proceed by anything of the sort.

But the point is here, that Malthus meant his argument as an argument against all social reform. He never thought of using it as anything else, except an argument against all social reform.

Nobody else ever thought in those more logical days of using it as anything but an argument against social reform. Malthus even used it as an argument against the ancient habit of human charity. He warned people against any generosity in the giving of alms. His theory was always thrown as cold water on any proposal to give the poor man property or a better status. Such is the noble story of the birth of Birth Control.

The only difference is this: that the old capitalists were more sincere and more scientific, while the modern capitalists are more hypocritical and more hazy. The rich man of 1850 used it in theory for the oppression of the poor. The rich man of 1927 will only use it in practice for the oppression of the poor. Being incapable of theory, being indeed incapable of thought, he can only deal in two things: what he calls practicality and what I call sentimentality. Not being so much of a man as Malthus, he cannot bear to be a pessimist, so he becomes a sentimentalist. He mixes up this old plain brutal idea (that the poor must be forbidden to breed) with a lot of slipshod and sickly social ideals and promises which are flatly incompatible with it. But he is after all a practical man, and he will be quite as brutal as his forbears when it comes to practice. And the practical upshot of the whole thing is plain enough. If he can prevent his servants from having families, he need not support those families Why the devil should he?

A Simple Test

If anybody doubts that this is the very simple motive, let him test it by the very simple statements made by the various Birth-Controllers like the Dean of St. Paul's. They never do say that we suffer from a too bountiful supply of bankers or that cosmopolitan financiers must not have such large families. They do not say that the fashionable throng at Ascot wants thinning, or that it is desirable to decimate the people dining at the Ritz or the Savoy. Though, Lord knows, if ever a thing human could look like a sub-human jungle, with tropical flowers and very poisonous weeds, it is the rich crowd that assembles in a modern Americanized hotel.

But the Birth-Controllers have not the smallest desire to control that jungle. It is much too dangerous a jungle to touch. It contains tigers. They never do talk about a danger from the comfortable classes, even from a more respectable section of the comfortable classes. The Gloomy Dean is not gloomy about there being too many Dukes; and naturally not about there being too many Deans. He is not primarily annoyed with a politician for having a whole population of poor relations, though places and public salaries have to be found for all the relations. Political Economy means that everybody except politicians must be economical.

The Birth-Controller does not bother about all these things, for the perfectly simple reason that it is not such people that he wants to control. What he wants to control is the populace, and he practically says so. He always insists that a workman has no right to have so many children, or that a slum is perilous because it is producing so many children. The question he dreads is "Why has not the workman a better wage? Why has not the slum family a better house?" His way of escaping from it is to suggest, not a larger house but a smaller family. The landlord or the employer says in his hearty and handsome fashion: "You really cannot expect me to deprive myself of my money. But I will make a sacrifice, I will deprive myself of your children."

One of a Class

Meanwhile, as the Malthusian attack on democratic hopes slowly stiffened and strengthened all the reactionary resistance to reform in this country, other forces were already in the field. I may remark in passing that Malthus, and his sophistry against all social reform, did not stand alone. It was one of a whole class of scientific excuses invented by the rich as reasons for denying justice to the poor, especially when the old superstitious glamour about kings and nobles had faded in the nineteenth century. One was talking about the Iron Laws of Political Economy, and pretending that somebody had proved somewhere, with figures on a slate, that injustice is incurable. Another was a mass of brutal nonsense about Darwinism and a struggle for life, in which the devil must catch the hindmost. As a fact it was struggle for wealth, in which the devil generally catches the foremost. They all had the character of an attempt to twist the new tool of science to make it a weapon for the old tyranny of money.

But these forces, though powerful in a diseased industrial plutocracy. were not the only forces even in the nineteenth century. Towards the end of that century, especially on the Continent, there was another movement going on, notably among Christian Socialists and those called Catholic Democrats and others. There is no space to describe it here; its interest lies in being the exact reversal of the order of argument used by the Malthusian and the Birth-Controller. This movement was not content with the test of what is called a Living Wage. It insisted specially on what it preferred to call a Family Wage. In other words, it maintained that no wage is just or adequate unless it does envisage and cover the man, not only considered as an individual, but as the father of a normal and reasonably numerous family. This sort of movement is the true contrary of Birth Control and both will probably grow until they come into some tremendous controversial collision. It amuses me to reflect on that big coming battle, and to remember that the more my opponents practise Birth Control, the fewer there will be of them to fight us on that day.

The Conflict

What I cannot get my opponents in this matter to see, in the strange mental confusion that covers the question, is the perfectly simple fact that these two claims, whatever else they are, are contrary claims. At the very beginning of the whole discussion stands the elementary fact that limiting families is a reason for lowering wages and not a reason for raising them. You may like the limitation for other reasons, as you may dislike it for other reasons. You may drag the discussion off to entirely different questions, such as, whether wives in normal homes are slaves. You may compromise out of consideration for the employer or for some other reason, and meet him half-way by taking half a loaf or having half a family. But the claims are in principle opposite. It is the whole truth in that theory of the class war about which the newspapers talk such nonsense. The full claim of the poor would be to have what they considered a full-sized family. If you cut this down to suit wages you make a concession to fit the capitalist conditions. The practical application I shall mention in a moment; I am talking now about the primary logical contradiction. If the two methods can be carried out, they can be carried out so as to contradict and exclude each other. One has no need of the other; one can dispense with or destroy the other. If you can make the wage larger, there is no need to make the family smaller. If you can make the family small, there is no need to make the wage larger. Anyone may judge which the ruling capitalist will probably prefer to do. But if he does one, he need not do the other.

There is of course a great deal more to be said. I have dealt with only one feature of Birth Control--its exceedingly unpleasant origin. I said it was purely capitalist and reactionary; I venture to say I have proved it was entirely capitalist and reactionary. But there are many other aspects of this evil thing. It is unclean in the light of the instincts; it is unnatural in relation to the affections; it is part of a general attempt to run the populace on a routine of quack medicine and smelly science; it is mixed up with a muddled idea that women are free when they serve their employers but slaves when they help their husbands; it is ignorant of the very existence of real households where prudence comes by free-will and agreement. It has all those aspects, and many of them would be extraordinarily interesting to discuss. But in order not to occupy too much space, I will take as a text nothing more than the title.

A Piece of Humbug

The very name of "Birth Control" is a piece of pure humbug. It is one of those blatant euphemisms used in the headlines of the Trust Press. It is like "Tariff Reform." It is like "Free Labour." It is meant to mean nothing, that it may mean anything, and especially some thing totally different from what it says. Everybody believes in birth control, and nearly everybody has exercised some control over the conditions of birth. People do not get married as somnambulists or have children in their sleep. But throughout numberless ages and nations, the normal and real birth control is called self control. If anybody says it cannot is possibly work, I say it does. In many classes, in many countries where these quack nostrums are unknown, populations of free men have remained within reasonable limits by sound traditions of thrift and responsibility. In so far as there is a local evil of excess, it comes with all other evils from the squalor and despair of our decaying industrialism. But the thing the capitalist newspapers call birth control is not control at all. It is the idea that people should be, in one respect, completely and utterly uncontrolled, so long as they can evade everything in the function that is positive and creative, and intelligent and worthy of a free man. It is a name given to a succession of different expedients, (the one that was used last is always described as having been dreadfully dangerous) by which it is possible to filch the pleasure belonging to a natural process while violently and unnaturally thwarting the process itself.

The nearest and most respectable parallel would be that of the Roman epicure, who took emetics at intervals all day so that he might eat five or six luxurious dinners daily. Now any man's common sense, unclouded by newspaper science and long words, will tell him at once that an operation like that of the epicures is likely in the long run even to be bad for his digestion and pretty certain to be bad for his character. Men left to themselves gave sense enough to know when a habit obviously savours of perversion and peril. And if it were the fashion in fashionable circles to call the Roman expedient by the name of "Diet Control," and to talk about it in a lofty fashion as merely "the improvement of life and the service of life" (as if it meant no more than the mastery of man over his meals), we should take the liberty of calling it cant and saying that it had no relation to the reality in debate.

The Mistake

The fact is, I think, that I am in revolt against the conditions of industrial capitalism and the advocates of Birth Control are in revolt against the conditions of human life. What their spokesmen can possibly mean by saying that I wage a "class war against mothers" must remain a matter of speculation. If they mean that I do the unpardonable wrong to mothers of thinking they will wish to continue to be mothers, even in a society of greater economic justice and civic equality, then I think they are perfectly right. I doubt whether mothers could escape from motherhood into Socialism. But the advocates of Birth Control seem to want some of them to escape from it into capitalism. They seem to express a sympathy with those who prefer "the right to earn outside the home" or (in other words) the right to be a wage-slave and work under the orders of a total stranger because he happens to be a richer man. By what conceivable contortions of twisted thought this ever came to be considered a freer condition than that of companionship with the man she has herself freely accepted, I never could for the life of me make out. The only sense I can make of it is that the proletarian work, though obviously more senile and subordinate than the parental, is so far safer and more irresponsible because it is not parental. I can easily believe that there are some people who do prefer working in a factory to working in a family; for there are always some people who prefer slavery to freedom, and who especially prefer being governed to governing someone else. But I think their quarrel with motherhood is not like mine, a quarrel with inhuman conditions, but simply a quarrel with life. Given an attempt to escape from the nature of things, and I can well believe that it might lead at last to something like "the nursery school for our children staffed by other mothers and single women of expert training."

I will add nothing to that ghastly picture, beyond speculating pleasantly about the world in which women cannot manage their own children but can manage each other's. But I think it indicates an abyss between natural and unnatural arrangements which would have to be bridged before we approached what is supposed to be the subject of discussion.

Appendix Two

G.K. Chesterton on the Family:

On Certain Modern Writers and the Institution of the Family / The Free Family / The Wildness of Domesticity / The Emancipation of Domesticity

[First selection from: *Heretics*, 1905, chapter 14; second, third, and fourth selections from: *What's Wrong With the World*, 1910, Part One: VII, VIII; Part Three: III]

ON CERTAIN MODERN WRITERS AND THE INSTITUTION OF THE FAMILY

The family may fairly be considered, one would think, an ultimate human institution. Every one would admit that it has been the main cell and central unit of almost all societies hitherto, except, indeed, such societies as that of Lacedaemon, which went in for "efficiency," and has, therefore, perished, and left not a trace behind. Christianity, even enormous as was its revolution, did not alter this ancient and savage sanctity; it merely reversed it. It did not deny the trinity of father, mother, and child. It merely read it backwards, making it run child, mother, father. This it called, not the family, but the Holy Family, for many things are made holy by being turned upside down. But some sages of our own decadence have made a serious attack on the family. They have impugned it, as I think wrongly; and its defenders have defended it, and defended it wrongly. The common defence of the family is that, amid the stress and fickleness of life, it is peaceful, pleasant, and at one. But there is another defence of the family which is possible, and to me evident; this defence is that the family is not peaceful and not pleasant and not at one.

It is not fashionable to say much nowadays of the advantages of the small community. We are told that we must go in for large empires and large ideas. There is one advantage, however, in the small state, the city, or the village, which only the wilfully blind can overlook. The man who lives in a small community lives in a much larger world. He knows much more of the fierce varieties and uncompromising divergences of men. The reason is obvious. In a large community we can choose our companions. In a small community our companions are chosen for us. Thus in all extensive and highly civilized societies groups come into existence founded upon what is called sympathy, and shut out the real world more sharply than the gates of a monastery. There is nothing really narrow about the clan; the thing which is really narrow is the clique. The men of the clan live together because they all wear the same tartan or are all descended from the same sacred cow; but in their souls, by the divine luck of things, there will always be more colours than in any tartan. But the men of the clique live together because they have the same kind of soul, and their narrowness is a narrowness of spiritual coherence and contentment, like that which exists in hell. A big society exists in order to form cliques. A big society is a society for the promotion of narrowness. It is a machinery for the purpose of guarding the solitary and sensitive individual from all experience of the bitter and bracing human compromises. It is, in the most literal sense of the words, a society for the prevention of Christian knowledge.

We can see this change, for instance, in the modern transformation of the thing called a club. When London was smaller, and the parts of London more self-contained and parochial, the club was what it still is in villages, the opposite of what it is now in great cities. Then the club was valued as a place where a man could be sociable. Now the club is valued as a place where a man can be unsociable. The more the enlargement and elaboration of our civilization goes on the more the club ceases to be a place where a man can have a noisy argument, and becomes more and more a place where a man can have what is somewhat fantastically called a quiet chop. Its aim is to make a man comfortable, and to make a man comfortable is to make him the opposite of sociable. Sociability, like all good things, is full of discomforts, dangers, and renunciations. The club tends to produce the most degraded of all combinations-- the luxurious anchorite, the man who combines the self-indulgence of Lucullus with the insane loneliness of St. Simeon Stylites.

If we were to-morrow morning snowed up in the street in which we live, we should step suddenly into a much larger and much wilder world than we have ever known. And it is the whole effort of the typically modern person to escape from the street in which he lives. First he invents modern hygiene and goes to Margate. Then he invents modern culture and goes to Florence. Then he invents modern imperialism and goes to Timbuctoo. He goes to the fantastic borders of the earth. He pretends to shoot tigers. He almost rides on a camel. And in all this he is still essentially fleeing from the street in which he was born; and of this flight he is always ready with his own explanation. He says he is fleeing from his street because it is dull; he is lying. He is really fleeing from his street because it is a great deal too exciting. It is exciting because it is exacting; it is exacting because it is alive. He can visit Venice because to him the Venetians are only Venetians; the people in his own street are men. He can stare at the Chinese because for him the Chinese are a passive thing to be stared at; if he stares at the old lady in the next garden, she becomes active. He is forced to flee, in short, from the too stimulating society of his equals--of free men, perverse, personal, deliberately different from himself. The street in Brixton is too glowing and overpowering. He has to soothe and quiet himself among tigers and vultures, camels and crocodiles. These creatures are indeed very different from himself. But they do not put their shape or colour or custom into a decisive intellectual competition with his own. They do not seek to destroy his principles and assert their own; the stranger monsters of the suburban street do seek to do this. The camel does not contort his features into a fine sneer because Mr. Robinson has not got a hump; the cultured gentleman at No. 5 does exhibit a sneer because Robinson has not got a dado. The vulture will not roar with laughter because a man does not fly; but the major at No. 9 will roar with laughter because a man does not smoke. The complaint we commonly have to make of our neighbours is that they will not, as we express it, mind their own business. We do not really mean that they will not mind their own business. If our neighbours did not mind their own business they would be asked abruptly for their rent, and would rapidly cease to be our neighbours. What we really mean when we say that they cannot mind their own business is something much deeper. We do not dislike them because they have so little force and fire that they cannot be interested in themselves. We dislike them because they have so much force and fire that they can be interested in us as well. What we dread about our neighbours, in short, is not the narrowness of their horizon, but their superb tendency to broaden it. And all aversions to ordinary humanity have this general character. They are not aversions to its feebleness (as is pretended), but to its energy. The misanthropes pretend that they despise humanity for its weakness. As a matter of fact, they hate it for its strength.

Of course, this shrinking from the brutal vivacity and brutal variety of common men is a perfectly reasonable and excusable thing as long as it does not pretend to any point of superiority. It is when it calls itself aristocracy or aestheticism or a superiority to the bourgeoisie that its inherent weakness has in justice to be pointed out. Fastidiousness is the most pardonable of vices; but it is the most unpardonable of virtues. Nietzsche, who represents most prominently this pretentious claim of the fastidious, has a description somewhere--a very powerful description in the purely literary sense--of the disgust and disdain which consume him at the sight of the common people with their common faces, their common voices, and their common minds. As I have said, this attitude is almost beautiful if we may regard it as pathetic. Nietzsche's aristocracy has about it all the sacredness that belongs to the weak. When he makes us feel that he cannot endure the innumerable faces, the incessant voices, the overpowering omnipresence which belongs to the mob, he will have the sympathy of anybody who has ever been sick on a steamer or tired in a crowded omnibus. Every man has hated mankind when he was less than a man. Every man has had humanity in his eyes like a blinding fog, humanity in his nostrils like a suffocating smell. But when Nietzsche has the incredible lack of humour and lack of imagination to ask us to believe that his aristocracy is an aristocracy of strong muscles or an aristocracy of strong wills, it is necessary to point out the truth. It is an aristocracy of weak nerves.

We make our friends; we make our enemies; but God makes our next-door neighbour. Hence he comes to us clad in all the careless terrors of nature; he is as strange as the stars, as reckless and indifferent as the rain. He is Man, the most terrible of the beasts. That is why the old religions and the old scriptural language showed so sharp a wisdom when they spoke, not of one's duty towards humanity, but one's duty towards one's neighbour. The duty towards humanity may often take the form of some choice which is personal or even pleasurable. That duty may be a hobby; it may even be a dissipation. We may work in the East End because we are peculiarly fitted to work in the East End, or because we think we are; we may fight for the cause of international peace because we are very fond of fighting. The most monstrous martyrdom, the most repulsive experience, may be the result of choice or a kind of taste. We may be so made as to be particularly fond of lunatics or specially interested in leprosy. We may love negroes because they are black or German Socialists because they are pedantic. But we have to love our neighbour because he is there-- a much more alarming reason for a much more serious operation. He is the sample of humanity which is actually given us. Precisely because he may be anybody he is everybody. He is a symbol because he is an accident.

Doubtless men flee from small environments into lands that are very deadly. But this is natural enough; for they are not fleeing from death. They are fleeing from life. And this principle applies to ring within ring of the social system of humanity. It is perfectly reasonable that men should seek for some particular variety of the human type, so long as they are seeking for that variety of the human type, and not for mere human variety. It is quite proper that a British diplomatist should seek the society of Japanese generals, if what he wants is Japanese generals. But if what he wants is people different from himself, he had much better stop at home and discuss religion with the housemaid. It is quite reasonable that the village genius should come up to conquer London if what he wants is to conquer London. But if he wants to conquer something fundamentally and symbolically hostile and also very strong, he had much better remain where he is and have a row with the rector. The man in the suburban street is quite right if he goes to Ramsgate for the sake of Ramsgate--a difficult thing to imagine. But if, as he expresses it, he goes to Ramsgate "for a change," then he would have a much more romantic and even melodramatic change if he jumped over the wall into his neighbours garden. The consequences would be bracing in a sense far beyond the possibilities of Ramsgate hygiene.

    Now, exactly as this principle applies to the empire, to the nation within the empire, to the city within the nation, to the street within the city, so it applies to the home within the street. The institution of the family is to be commended for precisely the same reasons that the institution of the nation, or the institution of the city, are in this matter to be commended. It is a good thing for a man to live in a family for the same reason that it is a good thing for a man to be besieged in a city. It is a good thing for a man to live in a family in the same sense that it is a beautiful and delightful thing for a man to be snowed up in a street. They all force him to realize that life is not a thing from outside, but a thing from inside. Above all, they all insist upon the fact that life, if it be a truly stimulating and fascinating life, is a thing which, of its nature, exists in spite of ourselves. The modern writers who have suggested, in a more or less open manner, that the family is a bad institution, have generally confined themselves to suggesting, with much sharpness, bitterness, or pathos, that perhaps the family is not always very congenial. Of course the family is a good institution because it is uncongenial. It is wholesome precisely because it contains so many divergencies and varieties. It is, as the sentimentalists say, like a little kingdom, and, like most other little kingdoms, is generally in a state of something resembling anarchy. It is exactly because our brother George is not interested in our religious difficulties, but is interested in the Trocadero Restaurant, that the family has some of the bracing qualities of the commonwealth. It is precisely because our uncle Henry does not approve of the theatrical ambitions of our sister Sarah that the family is like humanity. The men and women who, for good reasons and bad, revolt against the family, are, for good reasons and bad, simply revolting against mankind. Aunt Elizabeth is unreasonable, like mankind. Papa is excitable, like mankind Our youngest brother is mischievous, like mankind. Grandpapa is stupid, like the world; he is old, like the world.

Those who wish, rightly or wrongly, to step out of all this, do definitely wish to step into a narrower world. They are dismayed and terrified by the largeness and variety of the family. Sarah wishes to find a world wholly consisting of private theatricals; George wishes to think the Trocadero a cosmos. I do not say, for a moment, that the flight to this narrower life may not be the right thing for the individual, any more than I say the same thing about flight into a monastery. But I do say that anything is bad and artificial which tends to make these people succumb to the strange delusion that they are stepping into a world which is actually larger and more varied than their own. The best way that a man could test his readiness to encounter the common variety of mankind would be to climb down a chimney into any house at random, and get on as well as possible with the people inside. And that is essentially what each one of us did on the day that he was born.

This is, indeed, the sublime and special romance of the family. It is romantic because it is a toss-up. It is romantic because it is everything that its enemies call it. It is romantic because it is arbitrary. It is romantic because it is there. So long as you have groups of men chosen rationally, you have some special or sectarian atmosphere. It is when you have groups of men chosen irrationally that you have men. The element of adventure begins to exist; for an adventure is, by its nature, a thing that comes to us. It is a thing that chooses us, not a thing that we choose. Falling in love has been often regarded as the supreme adventure, the supreme romantic accident. In so much as there is in it something outside ourselves, something of a sort of merry fatalism, this is very true. Love does take us and transfigure and torture us. It does break our hearts with an unbearable beauty, like the unbearable beauty of music. But in so far as we have certainly something to do with the matter; in so far as we are in some sense prepared to fall in love and in some sense jump into it; in so far as we do to some extent choose and to some extent even judge--in all this falling in love is not truly romantic, is not truly adventurous at all. In this degree the supreme adventure is not falling in love. The supreme adventure is being born. There we do walk suddenly into a splendid and startling trap. There we do see something of which we have not dreamed before. Our father and mother do lie in wait for us and leap out on us, like brigands from a bush. Our uncle is a surprise. Our aunt is, in the beautiful common expression, a bolt from the blue. When we step into the family, by the act of being born, we do step into a world which is incalculable, into a world which has its own strange laws, into a world which could do without us, into a world that we have not made. In other words, when we step into the family we step into a fairy-tale.

This colour as of a fantastic narrative ought to cling to the family and to our relations with it throughout life. Romance is the deepest thing in life; romance is deeper even than reality. For even if reality could be proved to be misleading, it still could not be proved to be unimportant or unimpressive. Even if the facts are false, they are still very strange. And this strangeness of life, this unexpected and even perverse element of things as they fall out, remains incurably interesting. The circumstances we can regulate may become tame or pessimistic; but the "circumstances over which we have no control" remain god-like to those who, like Mr. Micawber, can call on them and renew their strength. People wonder why the novel is the most popular form of literature; people wonder why it is read more than books of science or books of metaphysics. The reason is very simple; it is merely that the novel is more true than they are. Life may sometimes legitimately appear as a book of science. Life may sometimes appear, and with a much greater legitimacy, as a book of metaphysics. But life is always a novel. Our existence may cease to be a song; it may cease even to be a beautiful lament. Our existence may not be an intelligible justice, or even a recognizable wrong. But our existence is still a story. In the fiery alphabet of every sunset is written, "to be continued in our next." If we have sufficient intellect, we can finish a philosophical and exact deduction, and be certain that we are finishing it right. With the adequate brain-power we could finish any scientific discovery, and be certain that we were finishing it right. But not with the most gigantic intellect could we finish the simplest or silliest story, and be certain that we were finishing it right. That is because a story has behind it, not merely intellect which is partly mechanical, but will, which is in its essence divine. The narrative writer can send his hero to the gallows if he likes in the last chapter but one. He can do it by the same divine caprice whereby he, the author, can go to the gallows himself, and to hell afterwards if he chooses. And the same civilization, the chivalric European civilization which asserted freewill in the thirteenth century, produced the thing called "fiction" in the eighteenth. When Thomas Aquinas asserted the spiritual liberty of man, he created all the bad novels in the circulating libraries.

But in order that life should be a story or romance to us, it is necessary that a great part of it, at any rate, should be settled for us without our permission. If we wish life to be a system, this may be a nuisance; but if we wish it to be a drama, it is an essential. It may often happen, no doubt, that a drama may be written by somebody else which we like very little. But we should like it still less if the author came before the curtain every hour or so, and forced on us the whole trouble of inventing the next act. A man has control over many things in his life; he has control over enough things to be the hero of a novel. But if he had control over everything, there would be so much hero that there would be no novel. And the reason why the lives of the rich are at bottom so tame and uneventful is simply that they can choose the events. They are dull because they are omnipotent. They fail to feel adventures because they can make the adventures. The thing which keeps life romantic and full of fiery possibilities is the existence of these great plain limitations which force all of us to meet the things we do not like or do not expect. It is vain for the supercilious moderns to talk of being in uncongenial surroundings. To be in a romance is to be in uncongenial surroundings. To be born into this earth is to be born into uncongenial surroundings, hence to be born into a romance. Of all these great limitations and frameworks which fashion and create the poetry and variety of life, the family is the most definite and important. Hence it is misunderstood by the moderns, who imagine that romance would exist most perfectly in a complete state of what they call liberty. They think that if a man makes a gesture it would be a startling and romantic matter that the sun should fall from the sky. But the startling and romantic thing about the sun is that it does not fall from the sky. They are seeking under every shape and form a world where there are no limitations--that is, a world where there are no outlines; that is, a world where there are no shapes. There is nothing baser than that infinity. They say they wish to be, as strong as the universe, but they really wish the whole universe as weak as themselves.

THE FREE FAMILY

As I have said, I propose to take only one central instance; I will take the institution called the private house or home; the shell and organ of the family. We will consider cosmic and political tendencies simply as they strike that ancient and unique roof. Very few words will suffice for all I have to say about the family itself. I leave alone the speculations about its animal origin and the details of its social reconstruction; I am concerned only with its palpable omnipresence. It is a necessity far mankind; it is (if you like to put it so) a trap for mankind. Only by the hypocritical ignoring of a huge fact can any one contrive to talk of "free love"; as if love were an episode like lighting a cigarette, or whistling a tune. Suppose whenever a man lit a cigarette, a towering genie arose from the rings of smoke and followed him everywhere as a huge slave. Suppose whenever a man whistled a tune he "drew an angel down" and had to walk about forever with a seraph on a string. These catastrophic images are but faint parallels to the earthquake consequences that Nature has attached to sex; and it is perfectly plain at the beginning that a man cannot be a free lover; he is either a traitor or a tied man. The second element that creates the family is that its consequences, though colossal, are gradual; the cigarette produces a baby giant, the song only an infant seraph. Thence arises the necessity for some prolonged system of co-operation; and thence arises the family in its full educational sense.

It may be said that this institution of the home is the one anarchist institution. That is to say, it is older than law, and stands outside the State. By its nature it is refreshed or corrupted by indefinable forces of custom or kinship. This is not to be understood as meaning that the State has no authority over families; that State authority is invoked and ought to be invoked in many abnormal cases. But in most normal cases of family joys and sorrows, the State has no mode of entry. It is not so much that the law should not interfere, as that the law cannot. Just as there are fields too far off for law, so there are fields too near; as a man may see the North Pole before he sees his own backbone. Small and near matters escape control at least as much as vast and remote ones; and the real pains and pleasures of the family form a strong instance of this. If a baby cries for the moon, the policeman cannot procure the moon--but neither can he stop the baby. Creatures so close to each other as husband and wife, or a mother and children, have powers of making each other happy or miserable with which no public coercion can deal. If a marriage could be dissolved every morning it would not give back his night's rest to a man kept awake by a curtain lecture; and what is the good of giving a man a lot of power where he only wants a little peace? The child must depend on the most imperfect mother; the mother may be devoted to the most unworthy children; in such relations legal revenges are vain. Even in the abnormal cases where the law may operate, this difficulty is constantly found; as many a bewildered magistrate knows. He has to save children from starvation by taking away their breadwinner. And he often has to break a wife's heart because her husband has already broken her head. The State has no tool delicate enough to deracinate the rooted habits and tangled affections of the family; the two sexes, whether happy or unhappy, are glued together too tightly for us to get the blade of a legal penknife in between them. The man and the woman are one flesh--yes, even when they are not one spirit. Man is a quadruped. Upon this ancient and anarchic intimacy, types of government have little or no effect; it is happy or unhappy, by its own sexual wholesomeness and genial habit, under the republic of Switzerland or the despotism of Siam. Even a republic in Siam would not have done much towards freeing the Siamese Twins.

The problem is not in marriage, but in sex; and would be felt under the freest concubinage. Nevertheless, the overwhelming mass of mankind has not believed in freedom in this matter, but rather in a more or less lasting tie. Tribes and civilizations differ about the occasions on which we may loosen the bond, but they all agree that there is a bond to be loosened, not a mere universal detachment. For the purposes of this book I am not concerned to discuss that mystical view of marriage in which I myself believe: the great European tradition which has made marriage a sacrament. It is enough to say here that heathen and Christian alike have regarded marriage as a tie; a thing not normally to be sundered. Briefly, this human belief in a sexual bond rests on a principle of which the modern mind has made a very inadequate study. It is, perhaps, most nearly paralleled by the principle of the second wind in walking.

The principle is this: that in everything worth having, even in every pleasure, there is a point of pain or tedium that must be survived, so that the pleasure may revive and endure. The joy of battle comes after the first fear of death; the joy of reading Virgil comes after the bore of learning him; the glow of the sea-bather comes after the icy shock of the sea bath; and the success of the marriage comes after the failure of the honeymoon. All human vows, laws, and contracts are so many ways of surviving with success this breaking point, this instant of potential surrender.

In everything on this earth that is worth doing, there is a stage when no one would do it, except for necessity or honor. It is then that the Institution upholds a man and helps him on to the firmer ground ahead. Whether this solid fact of human nature is sufficient to justify the sublime dedication of Christian marriage is quite an other matter, it is amply sufficient to justify the general human feeling of marriage as a fixed thing, dissolution of which is a fault or, at least, an ignominy. The essential element is not so much duration as security. Two people must be tied together in order to do themselves justice; for twenty minutes at a dance, or for twenty years in a marriage. In both cases the point is, that if a man is bored in the first five minutes he must go on and force himself to be happy. Coercion is a kind of encouragement; and anarchy (or what some call liberty) is essentially oppressive, because it is essentially discouraging. If we all floated in the air like bubbles, free to drift anywhere at any instant, the practical result would be that no one would have the courage to begin a conversation. It would be so embarrassing to start a sentence in a friendly whisper, and then have to shout the last half of it because the other party was floating away into the free and formless ether The two must hold each other to do justice to each other. If Americans can be divorced for "incompatibility of temper" I cannot conceive why they are not all divorced. I have known many happy marriages, but never a compatible one. The whole aim of marriage is to fight through and survive the instant when incompatibility becomes unquestionable. For a man and a woman, as such, are incompatible.

THE WILDNESS OF DOMESTICITY

In the course of this crude study we shall have to touch on what is called the problem of poverty, especially the dehumanized poverty of modern industrialism. But in this primary matter of the ideal the difficulty is not the problem of poverty, but the problem of wealth. It is the special psychology of leisure and luxury that falsifies life. Some experience of modern movements of the sort called "advanced" has led me to the conviction that they generally repose upon some experience peculiar to the rich. It is so with that fallacy of free love of which I have already spoken; the idea of sexuality as a string of episodes. That implies a long holiday in which to get tired of one woman, and a motor car in which to wander looking for others; it also implies money for maintenances. An omnibus conductor has hardly time to love his own wife, let alone other people's. And the success with which nuptial estrangements are depicted in modern "problem plays" is due to the fact that there is only one thing that a drama cannot depict--that is a hard day's work. I could give many other instances of this plutocratic assumption behind progressive fads. For instance, there is a plutocratic assumption behind the phrase "Why should woman be economically dependent upon man?" The answer is that among poor and practical people she isn't; except in the sense in which he is dependent upon her. A hunter has to tear his clothes; there must be somebody to mend them. A fisher has to catch fish; there must be somebody to cook them. It is surely quite clear that this modern notion that woman is a mere "pretty clinging parasite," "a plaything," etc., arose through the somber contemplation of some rich banking family, in which the banker, at least, went to the city and pretended to do something, while the banker's wife went to the Park and did not pretend to do anything at all. A poor man and his wife are a business partnership. If one partner in a firm of publishers interviews the authors while the other interviews the clerks, is one of them economically dependent? Was Hodder a pretty parasite clinging to Stoughton? Was Marshall a mere plaything for Snelgrove?

But of all the modern notions generated by mere wealth the worst is this: the notion that domesticity is dull and tame. Inside the home (they say) is dead decorum and routine; outside is adventure and variety. This is indeed a rich man's opinion. The rich man knows that his own house moves on vast and soundless wheels of wealth, is run by regiments of servants, by a swift and silent ritual. On the other hand, every sort of vagabondage of romance is open to him in the streets outside. He has plenty of money and can afford to be a tramp. His wildest adventure will end in a restaurant, while the yokel's tamest adventure may end in a police-court. If he smashes a window he can pay for it; if he smashes a man he can pension him. He can (like the millionaire in the story) buy an hotel to get a glass of gin. And because he, the luxurious man, dictates the tone of nearly all "advanced" and "progressive" thought, we have almost forgotten what a home really means to the overwhelming millions of mankind.

For the truth is, that to the moderately poor the home is the only place of liberty. Nay, it is the only place of anarchy. It is the only spot on the earth where a man can alter arrangements suddenly, make an experiment or indulge in a whim. Everywhere else he goes he must accept the strict rules of the shop, inn, club, or museum that he happens to enter. He can eat his meals on the floor in his own house if he likes. I often do it myself; it gives a curious, childish, poetic, picnic feeling. There would be considerable trouble if I tried to do it in an A.B.C. tea-shop. A man can wear a dressing gown and slippers in his house; while I am sure that this would not be permitted at the Savoy, though I never actually tested the point. If you go to a restaurant you must drink some of the wines on the wine list, all of them if you insist, but certainly some of them. But if you have a house and garden you can try to make hollyhock tea or convolvulus wine if you like. For a plain, hard-working man the home is not the one tame place in the world of adventure. It is the one wild place in the world of rules and set tasks. The home is the one place where he can put the carpet on the ceiling or the slates on the floor if he wants to. When a man spends every night staggering from bar to bar or from music-hall to music-hall, we say that he is living an irregular life. But he is not; he is living a highly regular life, under the dull, and often oppressive, laws of such places. Some times he is not allowed even to sit down in the bars; and frequently he is not allowed to sing in the music-halls. Hotels may be defined as places where you are forced to dress; and theaters may be defined as places where you are forbidden to smoke. A man can only picnic at home.

Now I take, as I have said, this small human omnipotence, this possession of a definite cell or chamber of liberty, as the working model for the present inquiry. Whether we can give every English man a free home of his own or not, at least we should desire it; and he desires it. For the moment we speak of what he wants, not of what he expects to get. He wants, far instance, a separate house; he does not want a semi-detached house. He may be forced in the commercial race to share one wall with another man. Similarly he might be forced in a three-legged race to share one leg with another man; but it is not so that he pictures himself in his dreams of elegance and liberty. Again, he does not desire a flat. He can eat and sleep and praise God in a flat; he can eat and sleep and praise God in a railway train. But a railway train is not a house, because it is a house on wheels. And a flat is not a house, because it is a house on stilts. An idea of earthy contact and foundation, as well as an idea of separation and independence, is a part of this instructive human picture.

I take, then, this one institution as a test. As every normal man desires a woman, and children born of a woman, every normal man desires a house of his own to put them into. He does not merely want a roof above him and a chair below him; he wants an objective and visible kingdom; a fire at which he can cook what food he likes, a door he can open to what friends he chooses. This is the normal appetite of men; I do not say there are not exceptions. There may be saints above the need and philanthropists below it. Opalstein, now he is a duke, may have got used to more than this; and when he was a convict may have got used to less. But the normality of the thing is enormous. To give nearly everybody ordinary houses would please nearly everybody; that is what I assert without apology. Now in modern England (as you eagerly point out) it is very difficult to give nearly everybody houses. Quite so; I merely set up the desideratum; and ask the reader to leave it standing there while he turns with me to a consideration of what really happens in the social wars of our time.

THE EMANCIPATION OF DOMESTICITY

And it should be remarked in passing that this force upon a man to develop one feature has nothing to do with what is commonly called our competitive system, but would equally exist under any rationally conceivable kind of Collectivism. Unless the Socialists are frankly ready for a fall in the standard of violins, telescopes and electric lights, they must somehow create a moral demand on the individual that he shall keep up his present concentration on these things. It was only by men being in some degree specialist that there ever were any telescopes; they must certainly be in some degree specialist in order to keep them going. It is not by making a man a State wage-earner that you can prevent him thinking principally about the very difficult way he earns his wages. There is only one way to preserve in the world that high levity and that more leisurely outlook which fulfils the old vision of universalism. That is, to permit the existence of a partly protected half of humanity; a half which the harassing industrial demand troubles indeed, but only troubles indirectly. In other words, there must be in every center of humanity one human being upon a larger plan; one who does not "give her best," but gives her all.

Our old analogy of the fire remains the most workable one. The fire need not blaze like electricity nor boil like boiling water; its point is that it blazes more than water and warms more than light. The wife is like the fire, or to put things in their proper proportion, the fire is like the wife. Like the fire, the woman is expected to cook: not to excel in cooking, but to cook; to cook better than her husband who is earning the coke by lecturing on botany or breaking stones. Like the fire, the woman is expected to tell tales to the children, not original and artistic tales, but tales-- better tales than would probably be told by a first-class cook. Like the fire, the woman is expected to illuminate and ventilate, not by the most startling revelations or the wildest winds of thought, but better than a man can do it after breaking stones or lecturing. But she cannot be expected to endure anything like this universal duty if she is also to endure the direct cruelty of competitive or bureaucratic toil. Woman must be a cook, but not a competitive cook; a school mistress, but not a competitive schoolmistress; a house-decorator but not a competitive house-decorator; a dressmaker, but not a competitive dressmaker. She should have not one trade but twenty hobbies; she, unlike the man, may develop all her second bests. This is what has been really aimed at from the first in what is called the seclusion, or even the oppression, of women. Women were not kept at home in order to keep them narrow; on the contrary, they were kept at home in order to keep them broad. The world outside the home was one mass of narrowness, a maze of cramped paths, a madhouse of monomaniacs. It was only by partly limiting and protecting the woman that she was enabled to play at five or six professions and so come almost as near to God as the child when he plays at a hundred trades. But the woman's professions, unlike the child's, were all truly and almost terribly fruitful; so tragically real that nothing but her universality and balance prevented them being merely morbid. This is the substance of the contention I offer about the historic female position. I do not deny that women have been wronged and even tortured; but I doubt if they were ever tortured so much as they are tortured now by the absurd modern attempt to make them domestic empresses and competitive clerks at the same time. I do not deny that even under the old tradition women had a harder time than men; that is why we take off our hats. I do not deny that all these various female functions were exasperating; but I say that there was some aim and meaning in keeping them various. I do not pause even to deny that woman was a servant; but at least she was a general servant.

  The shortest way of summarizing the position is to say that woman stands for the idea of Sanity; that intellectual home to which the mind must return after every excursion on extravagance. The mind that finds its way to wild places is the poet's; but the mind that never finds its way back is the lunatic's. There must in every machine be a part that moves and a part that stands still; there must be in everything that changes a part that is unchangeable. And many of the phenomena which moderns hastily condemn are really parts of this position of the woman as the center and pillar of health. Much of what is called her subservience, and even her pliability, is merely the subservience and pliability of a universal remedy; she varies as medicines vary, with the disease. She has to be an optimist to the morbid husband, a salutary pessimist to the happy-go-lucky husband. She has to prevent the Quixote from being put upon, and the bully from putting upon others. The French King wrote--

"Toujours femme varie Bien fol qui s'y fie,"

but the truth is that woman always varies, and that is exactly why we always trust her. To correct every adventure and extravagance with its antidote in common-sense is not (as the moderns seem to think) to be in the position of a spy or a slave. It is to be in the position of Aristotle or (at the lowest) Herbert Spencer, to be a universal morality, a complete system of thought. The slave flatters; the complete moralist rebukes. It is, in short, to be a Trimmer in the true sense of that honorable term; which for some reason or other is always used in a sense exactly opposite to its own. It seems really to be supposed that a Trimmer means a cowardly person who always goes over to the stronger side. It really means a highly chivalrous person who always goes over to the weaker side; like one who trims a boat by sitting where there are few people seated. Woman is a trimmer; and it is a generous, dangerous and romantic trade.

The final fact which fixes this is a sufficiently plain one. Supposing it to be conceded that humanity has acted at least not unnaturally in dividing itself into two halves, respectively typifying the ideals of special talent and of general sanity (since they are genuinely difficult to combine completely in one mind), it is not difficult to see why the line of cleavage has followed the line of sex, or why the female became the emblem of the universal and the male of the special and superior. Two gigantic facts of nature fixed it thus: first, that the woman who frequently fulfilled her functions literally could not be specially prominent in experiment and adventure; and second, that the same natural operation surrounded her with very young children, who require to be taught not so much anything as everything. Babies need not to be taught a trade, but to be introduced to a world. To put the matter shortly, woman is generally shut up in a house with a human being at the time when he asks all the questions that there are, and some that there aren't. It would be odd if she retained any of the narrowness of a specialist. Now if anyone says that this duty of general enlightenment (even when freed from modern rules and hours, and exercised more spontaneously by a more protected person) is in itself too exacting and oppressive, I can understand the view. I can only answer that our race has thought it worth while to cast this burden on women in order to keep common-sense in the world. But when people begin to talk about this domestic duty as not merely difficult but trivial and dreary, I simply give up the question. For I cannot with the utmost energy of imagination conceive what they mean. When domesticity, for instance, is called drudgery, all the difficulty arises from a double meaning in the word. If drudgery only means dreadfully hard work, I admit the woman drudges in the home, as a man might drudge at the Cathedral of Amiens or drudge behind a gun at Trafalgar. But if it means that the hard work is more heavy because it is trifling, colorless and of small import to the soul, then as I say, I give it up; I do not know what the words mean. To be Queen Elizabeth within a definite area, deciding sales, banquets, labors and holidays; to be Whiteley within a certain area, providing toys, boots, sheets cakes. and books, to be Aristotle within a certain area, teaching morals, manners, theology, and hygiene; I can understand how this might exhaust the mind, but I cannot imagine how it could narrow it. How can it be a large career to tell other people's children about the Rule of Three, and a small career to tell one's own children about the universe? How can it be broad to be the same thing to everyone, and narrow to be everything to someone? No; a woman's function is laborious, but because it is gigantic, not because it is minute I will pity Mrs. Jones for the hugeness of her task; I will never pity her for its smallness.

But though the essential of the woman's task is universality, this does not, of course, prevent her from having one or two severe though largely wholesome prejudices. She has, on the whole, been more conscious than man that she is only one half of humanity; but she has expressed it (if one may say so of a lady) by getting her teeth into the two or three things which she thinks she stands for. I would observe here in parenthesis that much of the recent official trouble about women has arisen from the fact that they transfer to things of doubt and reason that sacred stubbornness only proper to the primary things which a woman was set to guard. One's own children, one's own altar, ought to be a matter of principle-- or if you like, a matter of prejudice. On the other hand, who wrote Junius's Letters ought not to be a principle or a prejudice, it ought to be a matter of free and almost indifferent inquiry. But take an energetic modern girl secretary to a league to show that George III wrote Junius, and in three months she will believe it, too, out of mere loyalty to her employers. Modern women defend their office with all the fierceness of domesticity. They fight for desk and typewriter as for hearth and home, and develop a sort of wolfish wifehood on behalf of the invisible head of the firm. That is why they do office work so well; and that is why they ought not to do it.

Appendix Three

G.K. Chesterton:

The Superstition of Divorce

[From: *The Superstition of Divorce*, 1920, I, II]

It is futile to talk of reform without reference to form. To take a case from my own taste and fancy, there is nothing I feel to be so beautiful and wonderful as a window. All casements are magic casements, whether they open on the foam or the front-garden; they lie close to the ultimate mystery and paradox of limitation and liberty. But if I followed my instinct towards an infinite number of windows, it would end in having no walls. It would also (it may be added incidentally) end in having no windows either; for a window makes a picture by making a picture-frame. But there is a simpler way of stating my more simple and fatal error. It is that I have wanted a window, without considering whether I wanted a house. Now many appeals are being made to us to-day on behalf of that light and liberty that might well be symbolised by windows; especially as so many of them concern the enlightenment and liberation of the house, in the sense of the home. Many quite disinterested people urge many quite reasonable considerations in the case of divorce, as a type of domestic liberation; but in the journalistic and general discussion of the matter there is far too much of the mind that works backwards and at random, in the manner of all windows and no walls. Such people say they want divorce, without asking themselves whether they want marriage. Even in order to be divorced it has generally been found necessary to go through the preliminary formality of being married; and unless the nature of this initial act be considered, we might as well be discussing haircutting for the bald or spectacles for the blind. To be divorced is to be in the literal sense unmarried; and there is no sense in a thing being undone when we do not know if it is done.

There is perhaps no worse advice, nine times out of ten, than the advice to do the work that's nearest. It is especially bad when it means, as it generally does, removing the obstacle that's nearest. It means that men are not to behave like men but like mice; who nibble at the thing that's nearest. The man, like the mouse, undermines what he cannot understand. Because he himself bumps into a thing, he calls it the nearest obstacle; though the obstacle may happen to he the pillar that holds up the whole roof over his head. He industriously removes the obstacle; and in return the, obstacle removes him, and much more valuable things than he. This opportunism is perhaps the most unpractical thing in this highly unpractical world. People talk vaguely against destructive criticism; but what is the matter with this criticism is not that it destroys, but that it does not criticise. It is destruction without design. It is taking a complex machine to pieces bit by bit, in any order, without even knowing what the machine is for. And if a man deals with a deadly dynamic machine on the principle of touching the knob that's nearest, he will find out the defects of that cheery philosophy. Now leaving many sincere and serious critics of modern marriage on one side for the moment, great masses of modern men and women, who write and talk about marriage, are thus nibbling blindly at it like an army of mice. When the reformers propose, for instance, that divorce should be obtainable after an absence of three years (the absence actually taken for granted in the first military arrangements of the late European War) their readers and supporters could seldom give any sort of logical reason for the period being three years, and not three months or three minutes. They are like people who should say "Give me three feet of dog"; and not care where the cut came. Such persons fail to see a dog as an organic entity; in other words, they cannot make head or tail of it. And the chief thing to say about such reformers of marriage is that they cannot make head or tail of it. They do not know what it is, or what it is meant to be, or what its supporters suppose it to be; they never look at it, even when they are inside it. They do the work that's nearest; which is poking holes in the bottom of a boat under the impression that they are digging in a garden. This question of what a thing is, and whether it is a garden or a boat, appears to them abstract and academic. They have no notion of how large is the idea they attack; or how relatively small appear the holes that they pick in it.

Thus, Sir Arthur Conan Doyle, an intelligent man in other matters, says that there is only a "theological" opposition to divorce, and that it is entirely founded on "certain texts" in the Bible about marriages. This is exactly as if he said that a belief in the brotherhood of men was only founded on certain texts in the Bible, about all men being the children of Adam and Eve. Millions of peasants and plain people all over the world assume marriage to be static, without having ever clapped eyes on any text. Numbers of more modern people, especially after the recent experiments in America, think divorce is a social disease, without having ever bothered about any text. It may be maintained that even in these, or in any one, the idea of marriage is ultimately mystical; and the same may be maintained about the idea of brotherhood. It is obvious that a husband and wife are not visibly one flesh, in the sense of being one quadruped. It is equally obvious that Paderewski and Jack Johnson are not twins, and probably have not played together at their mother's knee. There is indeed a very important admission, or addition, to be realised here. What is true is this: that if the nonsense of Nietzsche or some such sophist submerged current culture, so that it was the fashion to deny the duties of fraternity; then indeed it might be found that the group which still affirmed fraternity was the original group in whose sacred books was the text about Adam and Eve. Suppose some Prussian professor has opportunely discovered that Germans and lesser men are respectively descended from two such very different monkeys that they are in no sense brothers, but barely cousins (German) any number of times removed. And suppose he proceeds to remove them even further with a hatchet, suppose he bases on this a repetition of the conduct of Cain, saying not so much "Am I my brother's keeper?" as "Is he really my brother?" And suppose this higher philosophy of the hatchet becomes prevalent in colleges and cultivated circles, as even more foolish philosophies have done. Then I agree it probably will be the Christian, the man who preserves the text about Cain, who will continue to assert that he is still the professor's brother; that he is still the professor's keeper. He may possibly add that, in his opinion, the professor seems to require a keeper.

And that is doubtless the situation in the controversies about divorce and marriage to-day. It is the Christian church which continues to hold strongly, when the world for some reason has weakened on it, what many others hold at other times. But even then it is barely picking up the shreds and scraps of the subject to talk about a reliance on texts. The vital point in the comparison is this: that human brotherhood means a whole view of life, held in the light of life, and defended, rightly or wrongly, by constant appeals to every aspect of life. The religion that holds it most strongly will hold it when nobody else holds it; that is quite true, and that some of us may be so perverse as to think a point in favour of the religion. But anybody who holds it at all will hold it as a philosophy, not hung on one text but on a hundred truths. Fraternity may be a sentimental metaphor; I may be suffering a delusion when I hail a Montenegrin peasant as my long lost brother. As a fact, I have my own suspicions about which of us it is that has got lost. But my delusion is not a deduction from one text, or from twenty; it is the expression of a relation that to me at least seems a reality. And what I should say about the idea of a brother, I should say about the idea of a wife.

It is supposed to be very unbusinesslike to begin at the beginning. It is called "abstract and academic principles with which we English, etc., etc." It is still in some strange way considered unpractical to open up inquiries about anything by asking what it is. I happen to have, however, a fairly complete contempt for that sort of practicality; for I know that it is not even practical. My ideal business man would not be one who planked down fifty pounds and said "Here is hard cash; I am a plain man;

it is quite indifferent to me whether I am paying a debt, or giving alms to a beggar, or buying a wild bull or a bathing machine." Despite the infectious heartiness of his tone, I should still, in considering the hard cash, say (like a cabman) "What's this?" I should continue to insist, priggishly, that it was a highly practical point what the money was; what it was supposed to stand for, to aim at or to declare; what was the nature of the transaction; or, in short, what the devil the man supposed he was doing. I shall therefore begin by asking, in an equally mystical manner, what in the name of God and the angels a man getting married supposes he is doing. I shall begin by asking what marriage is; and the mere question will probably reveal that the act itself, good or bad, wise or foolish, is of a certain kind; that it is not an inquiry or an experiment or an accident; it may probably dawn on us that it is a promise. It can be more fully defined by saying it is a vow.

Many will immediately answer that it is a rash vow. I am content for the moment to reply that all vows are rash vows. I am not now defending but defining wows; I am pointing out that this is a discussion about vows; first, of whether there ought to be vows; and second, of what vows ought to be. Ought a man to break a promise? Ought a man to make a promise? These are philosophic questions; but the philosophic peculiarity of divorce and re-marriage, as compared with free love and no marriage, is that a man breaks and makes a promise at the same moment. It is a highly German philosophy; and recalls the way in which the enemy wishes to celebrate his successful destruction of all treaties by signing some more. If I were breaking a promise, I would do it without promises. But I am very far from minimising the momentous and disputable nature of the vow itself. I shall try to show, in a further article, that this rash and romantic operation is the only furnace from which can come the plain hardware of humanity, the cast-iron resistance of citizenship or the cold steel of common sense; but I am not denying that the furnace is a fire. The vow is a violent and unique thing; though there have been many besides the marriage vow; vows of chivalry, vows of poverty, vows of celibacy, pagan as well as Christian. But modern fashion has rather fallen out of the habit; and men miss the type for the lack of the parallels. The shortest way of putting the problem is to ask whether being free includes being free to bind oneself. For the vow is a tryst with oneself.

I may be misunderstood if I say, for brevity, that marriage is an affair of honour. The sceptic will be delighted to assent, by saying it is a fight. And so it is, if only with oneself; but the point here is that it necessarily has the touch of the heroic, in which virtue can be translated by virtus. Now about fighting, in its nature, there is an implied infinity or at least a potential infinity. I mean that loyalty in war is loyalty in defeat or even disgrace; it is due to the flag precisely at the moment when the flag nearly falls. We do already apply this to the flag of the nation; and the question is whether it is wise or unwise to apply it to the flag of the family. Of course, it is tenable that we should apply it to neither; that misgovernment in the nation or misery in the citizen would make the desertion of the flag an act of reason and not treason. I will only say here that, if this were really the limit of national loyalty, some of us would have deserted our nation long ago.

To the two or three articles appearing here on this subject I have given the title of the Superstition of Divorce; and the title is not taken at random. While free love seems to me a heresy, divorce does really seem to me a superstition. It is not only more of a superstition than free love, but much more of a superstition than strict sacramental marriage; and this point can hardly be made too plain. It is the partisans of divorce, not the defenders of marriage, who attach a stiff and senseless sanctity to a mere ceremony, apart from the meaning of the ceremony. It is our opponents, and not we, who hope to be saved by the letter of ritual, instead of the spirit of reality. It is they who hold that vow or violation, loyalty or disloyalty, can all be disposed of by a mysterious and magic rite, performed first in a law-court and then in a church or a registry office. There is little difference between the two parts of the ritual; except that the law court is much more ritualistic. But the plainest parallels will show anybody that all this is sheer barbarous credulity. It may or may not be superstition for a man to believe he must kiss the Bible to show he is telling the truth. It is certainly the most grovelling superstition for him to believe that, if he kisses the Bible, anything he says will come true. It would surely be the blackest and most benighted Bible-worship to suggest that the mere kiss on the mere book alters the moral quality of perjury. Yet this is precisely what is implied in saying that formal re-marriage alters the moral quality of conjugal infidelity. It may have been a mark of the Dark Ages that Harold should swear on a relic, though he were afterwards forsworn. But surely those ages would have been at their darkest, if he had been content to be sworn on a relic and forsworn on another relic. Yet this is the new altar these reformers would erect for us, out of the mouldy and meaningless relics of their dead law and their dying religion.

Now we, at any rate, are talking about an idea, a thing of the intellect and the soul; which we feel to be unalterable by legal antics. We are talking about the idea of loyalty; perhaps a fantastic, perhaps only an unfashionable idea, but one we can explain and defend as an idea. Now I have already pointed out that most sane men do admit our ideal in such a case as patriotism or public spirit; the necessity of saving the state to which we belong. The patriot may revile but must not renounce his country; he must curse it to cure it, but not to wither it up. The old pagan citizens felt thus about the city; and modern nationalists feel thus about the nation. But even mere modern internationalists feel it about something; if it is only the nation of mankind. Even the humanitarian does not become a misanthrope and live in a monkey-house. Even a disappointed Collectivist or Communist does not retire into the exclusive society of beavers, because beavers are all communists of the most class-conscious solidarity. He admits the necessity of clinging to his fellow creatures, and begging them to abandon the use of the possessive pronoun; heart-breaking as his efforts must seem to him after a time. Even a Pacifist does not prefer rats to men, on the ground that the rat community is so pure from the taint of Jingoism as always to leave the sinking ship. In short, everybody recognises that there is some ship, large and small, which he ought not to leave, even when he thinks it is sinking.

We may take it then that there are institutions to which we are attached finally; just as there are others to which we are attached temporarily. We go from shop to shop trying to get what we want; but we do not go from nation to nation doing this; unless we belong to a certain group now heading very straight for Pogroms. In the first case it is the threat that we shall withdraw our custom; in the second it is the threat that we shall never withdraw ourselves; that we shall be part of the institution to the last. The time when the shop loses its customers is the time when the city needs its citizens; but it needs them as critics who will always remain to criticise. I need not now emphasise the deadly need of this double energy of internal reform and external defence; the whole towering tragedy which has eclipsed our earth in our time is but one terrific illustration of it. The hammer-strokes are coming thick and fast now; and filling the world with infernal thunders; and there is still the iron sound of something unbreakable deeper and louder than all the things that break. We may curse the kings, we may distrust the captains, we may murmur at the very existence of the armies; but we know that in the darkest days that may come to us, no man will desert the flag.

Now when we pass from loyalty to the nation to loyalty to the family, there can be no doubt about the first and plainest difference. The difference is that the family is a thing far more free. The vow is a voluntary loyalty; and the marriage vow is marked among ordinary oaths of allegiance by the fact that the allegiance is also a choice. The man is not only a citizen of the city, but also the founder and builder of the city. He is not only a soldier serving the colours, but he has himself artistically selected and combined the colours, like the colours of an individual dress. If it be admissible to ask him to be true to the commonwealth that has made him, it is at least not more illiberal to ask him to be true to the commonwealth he has himself made. If civic fidelity be, as it is, a necessity, it is also in a special sense a constraint. The old joke against patriotism, the Gilbertian irony, congratulated the Englishman on his fine and fastidious taste in being born in England. It made a plausible point in saying "For he might have been a Russian"; though indeed we have liked to see some persons who seemed to think they could be Russians when the fancy took them. If commonsense considers even such involuntary loyalty natural, we can hardly wonder if it thinks voluntary loyalty still more natural. And the small state founded on the sexes is at once the most voluntary and the most natural of all self-governing states. It is not true of Mr. Brown that he might have been a Russian; but it may be true of Mrs. Brown that she might have been a Robinson.

Now it is not at all hard to see why this small community, so specially free touching its cause, should yet be specially bound touching its effects. It is not hard to see why the vow made most freely is the vow kept most firmly. There are attached to it, by the nature of things, consequences so tremendous that no contract can offer any comparison. There is no contract, unless it be what said to be signed in blood, that can call spirits from the vastly deep, or bring cherubs (or goblins) to inhabit a small modern villa. There is no stroke of the pen which creates real bodies and souls, or makes the characters in a novel come to life. The institution that puzzles intellectuals so much can be explained by the mere material fact (perceptible even to intellectuals) that children are, generally speaking, younger than their parents. "Till death do us part" is not an irrational formula, for those will almost certainly die before they see more than half of the amazing (or alarming) thing they have done.

Such is, in a curt and crude outline, this obvious thing for those to whom it is not obvious. Now I know there are thinking men among those who would tamper with it; and I shall expect some of these to reply to my questions But for the moment I only ask this question: whether the parliamentary and journalistic divorce movement shows even a shadowy trace of these fundamental truths, regarded as tests. Does it even discuss the nature of a vow, the limits and objects of loyalty, the survival of the family as a small and free state? The writers are content to say that Mr. Brown is uncomfortable with Mrs. Brown, and the last emancipation, for separated couples, seems only to mean that he is still uncomfortable without Mrs. Brown. These are not days in which being uncomfortable is felt as the final test of public action. For the rest, the reformers show statistically that families are in fact so scattered in our industrial anarchy, that they may as well abandon hope of finding their way home again. I am acquainted with that argument for making bad worse and I see it everywhere leading to slavery. Because London Bridge is broken down, we must assume that bridges are not meant to bridge. Because London commercialism and capitalism have copied hell, we are to continue to copy them. Anyhow, some will retain the conviction that the ancient bridge built between the two towers of sex is the worthiest of the great works of the earth.

It is exceedingly characteristic of the dreary decades before the War that the forms of freedom in which they seemed to specialise were suicide and divorce. I am not at the moment pronouncing on the moral problem of either; I am merely noting, as signs of those times, those two true or false counsels of despair; the end of life and the end of love. Other forms of freedom were being increasingly curtailed. Freedom indeed was the one thing that progressives and conservatives alike contemned. Socialists were largely concerned to prevent strikes, by State arbitration; that is, by adding another rich man to give the casting vote between rich and poor. Even in claiming what they called the right to work they tacitly surrendered the right to leave off working. Tories were preaching conscription, not so much to defend the independence of England as to destroy the independence of Englishmen. Liberals, of course, were chiefly interested in eliminating liberty, especially touching beer and betting. It was wicked to fight, and unsafe even to argue; for citing any certain and contemporary fact might land one in a libel action. As all these doors were successfully shut in our faces along the chilly and cheerless corridor of progress (with its glazed tiles) the doors of death and divorce alone stood open, or rather opened wider and wider. I do not expect the exponents of divorce to admit any similarity in the two things; yet the passing parallel is not irrelevant. It may enable them to realise the limits within which our moral instincts can, even for the sake of argument, treat this desperate remedy as a normal object of desire. Divorce is for us at best a failure, of which we are more concerned to find and cure the cause than to complete the effects; and we regard a system that produces many divorces as we do a system that drives men to drown and shoot themselves. For instance, it is perhaps the commonest complaint against the existing law that the poor cannot afford to avail themselves of it.

It is an argument to which normally I should listen with special sympathy. But while I should condemn the law being a luxury, my first thought will naturally be that divorce and death are only luxuries in a rather rare sense. I should not primarily condole with the poor man on the high price of prussic acid; or on the fact that all precipices of suitable suicidal height were the private property of the landlords. There are other high prices and high precipices I should attack first. I should admit in the abstract that what is sauce for the goose is sauce for the gander; that what is good for the rich is good for the poor; but my first and strongest impression would be that prussic acid sauce is not good for anybody. I fear I should, on the impulse of the moment, pull a poor clerk or artisan back by the coat-tails, if he were jumping over Shakespeare's Cliff, even if Dover sands were strewn with the remains of the dukes and bankers who had already taken the plunge.

But in one respect, I will heartily concede, the cult of divorce has differed from the mere cult of death. The cult of death is dead Those I knew in my youth as young pessimists are now aged optimists. And, what is more to the point at present, even when it was living it was limited; it was a thing of one clique in one class. We know the rule in the old comedy, that when the heroine went mad in white satin, the confidante went mad in white muslin. But when, in some tragedy of the artistic temperament, the painter committed suicide in velvet, it was never implied that the plumber must commit suicide in corduroy. It was never held that Hedda Walter's housemaid must die in torments on the carpet (trying as her term of service may have been); or that Mrs. Tanqueray's butler must play the Roman fool and die on his own carving knife. That particular form of playing the fool, Roman or otherwise, was an oligarchic privilege in the decadent epoch; and even as such has largely passed with that epoch. Pessimism, which was never popular, is no longer even fashionable. A far different fate has awaited the other fashion; the other somewhat dismal form of freedom. If divorce is a disease, it is no longer to be a fashionable disease like appendicitis; it is to be made an epidemic like small-pox. As we have already seen papers and public men to-day make a vast parade of the necessity of setting the poor man free to get a divorce. Now why are they so mortally anxious that he should be free to get a divorce, and not in the least anxious that he should be free to get anything else? Why are the same people happy, nay almost hilarious, when he gets a divorce, who are horrified when he gets a drink? What becomes of his money, what becomes of his children, where he works, when he ceases to work, are less and less under his personal control. Labour Exchanges, Insurance Cards, Welfare Work, and a hundred forms of police inspection and supervision have combined for good or evil to fix him more and more strictly to a certain place in society. He is less and less allowed to go to look for a new job; why is he allowed to go to look for a new wife? He is more and more compelled to recognise a Moslem code about liquor; why is it made so easy for him to escape from his old Christian code about sex? What is the meaning of this mysterious immunity, this special permit for adultery; and why is running away with his neighbour's wife to be the only exhilaration still left open to him? Why must he love as he pleases; when he may not even live as he pleases?

  The answer is, I regret to say, that this social campaign, in most though by no means all of its most prominent campaigners, relies in this matter on a very smug and pestilent piece of chalk. There are some advocates of democratic divorce who are really advocates of general democratic freedom; but they are the exceptions; I might say, with all respect, that they are the dupes. The omnipresence of the thing in the press and in political society is due to a motive precisely opposite to the motive professed. The modern rulers, who are simply the rich men, are really quite consistent in their attitude to the poor man. It is the same spirit which takes away his children under the pretence of order, which takes away his wife under the pretence of liberty. That which wishes, in the words of the comic song, to break up the happy home, is primarily anxious not to break up the much more unhappy factory. Capitalism, of course, is at war with the family, for the same reason which has led to its being at war with the Trade Union. This indeed is the only sense in which it is true that capitalism is connected with individualism. Capitalism believes in collectivism for itself and individualism for its enemies. It desires its victims to be individuals, or (in other words) to be atoms. For the word atom, in its clearest meaning (which is none too clear) might be translated as "individual." If there be any bond, if there be any brotherhood, if there be any class loyalty or domestic discipline, by which the poor can help the poor, these emancipators will certainly strive to loosen that bond or lift that discipline in the most liberal fashion. If there be such a brotherhood, these individualists will redistribute it in the form of individuals; or in other words smash it to atoms.

The masters of modern plutocracy know what they are about. They are making no mistake; they can be cleared of the slander of inconsistency. A very profound and precise instinct has let them to single out the human household as the chief obstacle to their inhuman progress. Without the family we are helpless before the State, which in our modern case is the Servile State. To use a military metaphor, the family is the only formation in which the charge of the rich can be repulsed. It is a force that forms twos as soldiers form fours; and, in every peasant country, has stood in the square house or the square plot of land as infantry have stood in squares against cavalry. How this force operates this, and why, I will try to explain in the last of these articles. But it is when it is most nearly ridden down by the horsemen of pride and privilege, as in Poland or Ireland, when the battle grows most desperate and the hope most dark, that men begin to understand why that wild oath in its beginnings was flung beyond the bonds of the world; and what would seem as passing as a vision is made permanent as a vow.

Appendix Four

1930 Lambeth Conference of Anglican Bishops: Resolutions : *The Life and Witness of the Christian Community - Marriage and Sex*

Resolution 9

The Conference believes that the conditions of modern life call for a fresh statement from the Christian Church on the subject of sex. It declares that the functions of sex as a God-given factor in human life are essentially noble and creative. Responsibility in regard to their right use needs the greater emphasis in view of widespread laxity of thought and conduct in all these matters.

Resolution 10

The Conference believes that in the exalted view of marriage taught by our Lord is to be found the solution of the problems with which we are faced. His teaching is reinforced by certain elements which have found a new emphasis in modern life, particularly the sacredness of personality, the more equal partnership of men and women, and the biological importance of monogamy.

Resolution 11

The Conference believes that it is with this ideal in view that the Church must deal with questions of divorce and with whatever threatens the security of women and the stability of the home. Mindful of our Lord's words, "What therefore God hath joined together, let not man put asunder," it reaffirms "as our Lord's principle and standard of marriage a life-long and indissoluble union, for better or worse, of one man with one woman, to the exclusion of all others on either side, and calls on all Christian people to maintain and bear witness to this standard." In cases of divorce:

> The Conference, while passing no judgement on the practice of regional or national Churches within our Communion, recommends that the marriage of one, whose former partner is still living, should not be celebrated according to the rites of the Church.
>
> Where an innocent person has remarried under civil sanction and desires to receive the Holy Communion, it recommends that the case should be referred for consideration to the bishop, subject to provincial regulations.
>
> Finally, it would call attention to the Church's unceasing responsibility for the spiritual welfare of all her members who have come short of her standard in this as in any other respect, and to the fact that the Church's aim, individually and socially, is reconciliation to God and redemption from sin. It therefore urges all bishops and clergy to keep this aim before them.

Resolution 12

In all questions of marriage and sex the Conference emphasises the need of education. It is important that before the child's emotional reaction to sex is awakened, definite information should be given in an atmosphere of simplicity and beauty. The persons directly responsible for this are the parents, who in the exercise of this responsibility will themselves need the best guidance that the Church can supply.

During childhood and youth the boy or the girl should thus be prepared for the responsibilities of adult life; but the Conference urges the need of some further preparation for those members of the Church who are about to marry.

To this end the Conference is convinced that steps ought to be taken:

to secure a better education for the clergy in moral theology;

to establish, where they do not exist, in the various branches of the Anglican Communion central councils which would study the problems of sex from the Christian standpoint and give advice to the responsible authorities in diocese or parish of theological college as to methods of approach and lines of instruction;

to review the available literature and to take steps for its improvement and its circulation.

Resolution 13

The Conference emphasises the truth that sexual instinct is a holy thing implanted by God in human nature. It acknowledges that intercourse between husband and wife as the consummation of marriage has a value of its own within that sacrament, and that thereby married love is enhanced and its character strengthened. Further, seeing that the primary purpose for which marriage exists is the procreation of children, it believes that this purpose as well as the paramount importance in married life of deliberate and thoughtful self-control should be the governing considerations in that intercourse.

Resolution 14

The Conference affirms:

the duty of parenthood as the glory of married life;

the benefit of a family as a joy in itself, as a vital contribution to the nation's welfare, and as a means of character-building for both parents and children;

the privilege of discipline and sacrifice to this end.

Resolution 15

Where there is clearly felt moral obligation to limit or avoid parenthood, the method must be decided on Christian principles. The primary and obvious method is complete abstinence from intercourse (as far as may be necessary) in a life of discipline and self-control lived in the power of the Holy Spirit. Nevertheless in those cases where there is such a clearly felt moral obligation to limit or avoid parenthood, and where there is a morally sound reason for avoiding complete abstinence, the Conference agrees that other methods may be used, provided that this is done in the light of the same Christian principles. The Conference records its strong condemnation of the use of any methods of conception control from motives of selfishness, luxury, or mere convenience.

[Voting: For 193; Against 67]

Resolution 16

The Conference further records its abhorrence of the sinful practice of abortion.

Resolution 17

While the Conference admits that economic conditions are a serious factor in the situation, it condemns the propaganda which treats conception control as a way of meeting those unsatisfactory social and economic conditions which ought to be changed by the influence of Christian public opinion.

Resolution 18

Sexual intercourse between persons who are not legally married is a grievous sin. The use of contraceptives does not remove the sin. In view of the widespread and increasing use of contraceptives among the unmarried and the extension of irregular unions owing to the diminution of any fear of consequences, the Conference presses for legislation forbidding the exposure for sale and the unrestricted advertisement of contraceptives, and placing definite restrictions upon their purchase.

Resolution 19

Fear of consequences can never, for the Christian, be the ultimately effective motive for the maintenance of chastity before marriage. This can only be found in the love of God and reverence for his laws. The Conference emphasises the need of strong and wise teaching to make clear the Christian standpoint in this matter. That standpoint is that all illicit and irregular unions are wrong in that they offend against the true nature of love, they compromise the future happiness of married life, they are antagonistic to the welfare of the community, and, above all, they are contrary to the revealed will of God.

Appendix Five

Subsequent Lambeth Conferences on Divorce, Contraception, Extramarital Sex, Homosexuality, the Ordination of Women, and Euthanasia

1948: Resolution 92: The Church's Discipline in Marriage [Divorce]

Faced with the great increase in the number of broken marriages and the tragedy of children deprived of true home life, this Conference desires again to affirm that marriage always entails a life-long union and obligation; it is convinced that upon the faithful observance of this divine law depend the stability of home life, the welfare and happiness of children, and the real health of society. It calls upon members of the Church and others to do their utmost by word and example to uphold the sanctity of the marriage bond and to counteract those influences which tend to destroy it. It is convinced that maintenance of the Church's standard of discipline can alone meet the deepest needs of men; and it earnestly implores those whose marriage, perhaps through no fault of their own, is unhappy to remain steadfastly faithful to their marriage vows.

1948: Resolution 94: The Church's Discipline in Marriage [Divorce]

The Conference affirms that the marriage of one whose former partner is still living may not be celebrated according to the rites of the Church, unless it has been established that there exists no marriage bond recognised by the Church.

1948: Resolution 97: The Church's Discipline in Marriage [Divorce]

Inasmuch as easy divorce in Great Britain, the United States, and elsewhere, has gravely weakened the idea of the life-long nature of marriage, and has also brought untold suffering to children, this Conference urges that there is a strong case for the reconsideration by certain states of their divorce laws.

1958: Resolution 114: The Family in Contemporary Society – Marriage [Divorce]

. . . special attention should be given to our Lord's principle of life-long union as the basis of all true marriage.

1958: Resolution 115: The Family in Contemporary Society – Marriage [Contraception]

The Conference believes that the responsibility for deciding upon the number and frequency of children has been laid by God upon the consciences of parents everywhere; that this planning, in such ways as are mutually acceptable to husband and wife in Christian conscience, is a right and important factor in Christian family life and should be the result of positive choice before God. Such responsible parenthood, built on obedience to all the duties of marriage, requires a wise stewardship of the resources and abilities of the family as well as a thoughtful consideration of the varying population needs and problems of society and the claims of future generations.

1958: Resolution 118: The Family in Contemporary Society – Marriage [Divorce]

The Conference recognises that divorce is granted by the secular authority in many lands on grounds which the Church cannot acknowledge, and recognises also that in certain cases where a decree of divorce has been sought and may even have been granted, there may in fact have been no marital bond in the eyes of the Church . . .

1958: Resolution 119: The Family in Contemporary Society – Marriage [Divorce]

The Conference believes that the Resolutions of the 1948 Lambeth Conference concerning marriage discipline have been of great value as witnessing to Christ's teaching about the life-long nature of marriage . . .

1968: Resolution 22: Responsible Parenthood [Contraception]

This Conference has taken note of the papal encyclical letter "Humanae vitae" recently issued by His Holiness Pope Paul VI. The Conference records its appreciation of the Pope's deep concern for the institution of marriage and the integrity of married life.
Nevertheless, the Conference finds itself unable to agree with the Pope's conclusion that all methods of conception control other than abstinence from sexual intercourse or its confinement to periods of infecundity are contrary to the "order established by God" . . .

1968: Resolution 34: The Ministry - Ordination of Women to the Priesthood [Women's Ordination as Priests]

The Conference affirms its opinion that the theological arguments as at present presented for and against the ordination of women to the priesthood are inconclusive.

1978: Resolution 21: Women in the Priesthood [Women's Ordination as Priests]

1. The Conference notes that since the last Lambeth Conference in 1968, the Diocese of Hong Kong, the Anglican

Church of Canada, the Episcopal Church in the United States of America, and the Church of the Province of New Zealand have admitted women to the presbyterate, and that eight other member Churches of the Anglican Communion have now either agreed or approved in principle or stated that there are either no fundamental or no theological objections to the ordination of women to the historic threefold ministry of the Church.

We also note that other of its member Churches have not yet made a decision on the matter. Others again have clearly stated that they do hold fundamental objections to the ordination of women to the historic threefold ministry of the Church . . .

6. . . . this Conference (a) declares its acceptance of those member Churches which now ordain women, and urges that they respect the convictions of those provinces and dioceses which do not; (b) declares its acceptance of those member Churches which do not ordain women, and urges that they respect the convictions of those provinces and dioceses which do . . .

7. We recognise that our accepting this variety of doctrine and practice in the Anglican Communion may disappoint the Roman Catholic, Orthodox, and Old Catholic Churches, but we wish to make it clear (a) that the holding together of diversity within a unity of faith and worship is part of the Anglican heritage; . . .

[Voting: For 316; Against 37; Abstentions 17]

1978: Resolution 22: Women in the Episcopate [Women's Ordination as Bishops]

While recognising that a member Church of the Anglican Communion may wish to consecrate women to the episcopate, and accepting that such member Church must act in accordance with its own constitution, the Conference recommends that no decision to consecrate be taken without consultation with the episcopate through the primates and overwhelming support in any member Church and in the diocese concerned, lest the bishop's office should become a cause of disunity instead of a focus of unity.

1988: Resolution 34: Marriage and Family [Extramarital Sex]

. . . 3. Noting the gap between traditional Christian teaching on pre-marital sex, and the life-styles being adopted by many people today, both within and outside the Church:
(a) calls on provinces and dioceses to adopt a caring and pastoral attitude to such people; (b) reaffirms the traditional biblical teaching that sexual intercourse is an act of total commitment which belongs properly within a permanent married relationship; (c) in response to the International Conference of Young Anglicans in Belfast, urges provinces and dioceses to plan with young people programmes to explore issues such as pre-marital sex in the light of traditional Christian values.

1998: Resolution 1:10: Human Sexuality [Divorce, Extramarital Sex, Homosexuality]

This Conference:
(a) commends to the Church the subsection report on human sexuality;
(b) in view of the teaching of Scripture, upholds faithfulness in marriage between a man and a woman in lifelong union, and believes that abstinence is right for those who are not called to marriage;
(c) recognises that there are among us persons who experience themselves as having a homosexual orientation. Many of these are members of the Church and are seeking the pastoral care, moral direction of the Church, and God's transforming power for the living of their lives and the ordering of relationships.
We commit ourselves to listen to the experience of homosexual persons and we wish to assure them that they are loved by God and that all baptised, believing and faithful persons, regardless of sexual orientation, are full members of the Body of Christ;

(d) while rejecting homosexual practice as incompatible with Scripture, calls on all our people to minister pastorally and sensitively to all irrespective of sexual orientation and to condemn irrational fear of homosexuals, violence within marriage and any trivialisation and commercialisation of sex;

(e) cannot advise the legitimising or blessing of same sex unions nor ordaining those involved in same gender unions; . . .

1998: Resolution 1.14: Euthanasia [Euthanasia]

In the light of current debate and proposals for the legalisation of euthanasia in several countries, this Conference:

(a) affirms that life is God-given and has intrinsic sanctity, significance and worth;

(b) defines euthanasia as the act by which one person intentionally causes or assists in causing the death of another who is terminally or seriously ill in order to end the other's pain and suffering;

(c) resolves that euthanasia, as precisely defined, is neither compatible with theChristian faith nor should be permitted in civil legislation;

(d) distinguishes between euthanasia and withholding, withdrawing, declining or terminating excessive medical treatment and intervention, all of which may be consonant with Christian faith in enabling a person to die with dignity. When a person is in a permanent vegetative state, to sustain him or her with artificial nutrition and hydration may be seen as constituting medical intervention; . . .

Appendix Six

Official Statements of Various Christian Denominations in Support of the Right to Abortion

[Information obtained from: *The Churches Speak on: Abortion: Official Statements from Religious Bodies and Ecumenical Organizations*, J. Gordon Melton, Gary L. Ward, Contributing Editor, Detroit: Gale Research Inc., 1989]

If you faint in the day of adversity, your strength is small. Rescue those who are being taken away to death . . . If you say, "Behold, we did not know this," does not he who weighs the heart perceive it? . . . and will he not requite man according to his work?

(Proverbs 24:10-12)

For they have committed adultery, and blood is upon their hands . . . . they have defiled my sanctuary . . . For when they had slaughtered their children in sacrifice to their idols, on the same day they came into my sanctuary to profane it . . .

(Ezekiel 23:37-39)

And you took your sons and your daughters, whom you had borne to me, and these you sacrificed . . .

(Ezekiel 16:20)

. . . Are you not children of transgression, the offspring of deceit, you who burn with lust among the oaks, . . . who slay your children in the valleys, under the clefts of the rocks?

(Isaiah 57:4-5)

How long will you judge unjustly and show partiality to the wicked? Give justice to the weak and the fatherless . . . Rescue the weak and needy; deliver them from the hand of the wicked.

(Psalm 82:2-4)

Therefore thou dost correct little by little those who trespass, and dost remind and warn them of the things wherein they sin, that they may be freed from wickedness and put their trust in thee, O Lord. Those who dwelt of old in thy holy land thou didst hate for their detestable practices . . . their merciless slaughter of children . . . these parents who murder helpless lives, thou didst will to destroy by the hands of our fathers.

(Wisdom 12:2-6)

"Not every one who says to me, 'Lord, Lord,' shall enter the kingdom of heaven, but he who does the will of my Father who is in heaven".

(Matthew 8:21)

The fetus, though enclosed in the womb of his mother, is already a human being, and it is a monstrous crime to rob it of life which it has not yet begun to enjoy. If it seems more horrible to kill a man in his own house tan in a field, because a man's house is his place of most secure refuge, it ought surely to be deemed more atrocious to destroy a fetus in the womb before it has come to light.

(John Calvin: *Commentaries on the Four Last Books of Moses*, translated by Charles William Bingham, Grand Rapids, MI: Eerdmans, 1950, vol. 3, 41-42; commentary on Exodus 21:22-23)

AMERICAN BAPTIST CHURCHES IN THE U.S.A. (1988)

. . . we encourage women and men in these circumstances to seek spiritual counsel as they prayerfully and conscientiously consider their decision . . . we are divided as to the proper witness of the church to the state regarding abortion . . . we acknowledge the freedom of each individual to advocate for a public policy on abortion that reflects his or her beliefs.

AMERICAN FRIENDS SERVICE COMMITTEE (QUAKERS) (1970)

. . . it is far better to end an unwanted pregnancy than to encourage the evils resulting from forced pregnancy and childbirth. At the center of our position is a profound respect and reverence for human life, not only that of the potential human being who should never have been conceived . . .

DISCIPLES OF CHRIST (1975)

[We] affirm the principle of religious liberty, freedom of individual conscience, and sacredness of life for all persons. [We] respect differences in religious beliefs concerning abortion and oppose, in accord with the principle of religious liberty, any attempt to legislate a specific religious opinion or belief concerning abortion upon all Americans.

EPISCOPAL CHURCH (1988)

All human life is sacred . . . while we acknowledge that in this country it is the legal right of every woman to have a medically safe abortion, as Christians we believe strongly that if this right is exercised, it should be used only in extreme situations . . . In those cases where an abortion is being considered, members of this Church are urged to seek the dictates of their consciences in prayer, to seek the advice and counsel of members of the Christian community . . . any proposed legislation . . . regarding abortions must take special care to see that individual conscience is respected . . .

EVANGELICAL LUTHERAN CHURCH IN AMERICA (1980)

. . . there may be circumstances when, all pertinent factors responsibly considered, an induced abortion may be a tragic option.

NATIONAL ASSOCIATION OF EVANGELICALS (1973)

. . . Other pregnancies, such as those resulting from rape or incest, may require deliberate termination . . .

PRESBYTERIAN CHURCH (U.S.A.) (1983)

[We] affirm women's ability to make responsible decisions, whether the choice be to abort or to carry the pregnancy to term.

REFORMED CHURCH IN AMERICA (1974)

. . . Scripture does not speak directly to the abortion issue . . . Scriptural passages often cited as determining the status of a human fetus as fully human, upon careful exegetical examination prove to be indecisive and not clearly supportive of an absolutist position, either affirmative or negative . . .

SALVATION ARMY (1986)

The Salvation Army believes in the sanctity of all human life . . . Termination of a pregnancy may be justified . . . in those instances of proven rape or legally defined incest or where reliable diagnostic procedures determine that a fetal anomaly is present . . .

UNITED CHURCH OF CANADA (1980)

As Christians we wish to affirm: The sanctity of human life, born or unborn . . . the taking of human life is evil . . . abortion is always a moral evil and can only be accepted as the lesser of two evils . . . prior to that stage of fetal development when abortion can no longer be performed by D & C suction, abortion should be a personal matter between a woman and her doctor . . . a free and responsive exercise of her conscience. After that period of time, abortion should only be performed following consultation with a second doctor . . . any interruption in the pregnancy is less objectionable in the early stages.

UNITED CHURCH OF CHRIST (1987)

Scripture teaches that all human life is precious in God's sight and teaches the importance of personal moral freedom . . . previous General Synods, beginning in 1971 . . . have supported its legal availability, while recognizing its moral ambiguity . . . the Sixteenth General Synod: Affirms the sacredness of all of life, and the need to protect and defend human life in particular; . . . Upholds the right of men and women . . . to safe, legal abortions as one option among others . . .

UNITED METHODIST CHURCH (1976; reaffirmed in 1988)

We support the legal right to abortion as established by the 1973 Supreme Court decision. We encourage women in counsel with husbands, doctors, and pastors to make their own responsible decisions concerning the personal and moral questions surrounding the issue of abortion.

UNITARIAN UNIVERSALIST ASSOCIATION (1987)

[We support] the right to choose contraception and abortion as legitimate aspects of the right to privacy . . . [and] actively oppose all legislation, regulation and administrative action, at any level of government, intended to undermine or circumvent the *Roe v. Wade* decision . . . [and] expose and oppose bogus clinics [i.e., crisis pregnancy centers] and other tactics that infringe on the free exercise of the right to choose . . .